LETTERS TO AN ATHEIST

LETTERS TO AN ATHEIST

Wrestling with Faith

PETER KREEFT

A Sheed & Ward Book

ROWMAN & LITTLEFIELD
Lanham • Boulder • New York • London

Published by Rowman & Littlefield
An imprint of The Rowman & Littlefield Publishing Group, Inc.
4501 Forbes Boulevard, Suite 200, Lanham, Maryland 20706
www.rowman.com

86-90 Paul Street, London EC2A 4NE

Distributed by NATIONAL BOOK NETWORK

British Library Cataloguing in Publication Information available

Library of Congress Cataloging-in-Publication Data

ISBN: 978-1-4422-3271-6 (cloth)
ISBN: 978-1-5381-8838-5 (paper)
ISBN: 978-1-4422-3272-3 (electronic)

♾™ The paper used in this publication meets the minimum requirements of
American National Standard for Information Sciences—Permanence of Paper
for Printed Library Materials, ANSI/NISO Z39.48-1992.

INTRODUCTION

These letters are real, and I invite real atheists to read and reply to them. (My email address is kreeft@bc.edu). The occasion for writing them that is mentioned in the first letter really happened. "Martha" and "Michael" are pseudonyms for real persons. I'm one too, I think. Even my cottage on Martha's Vineyard (mentioned in the last letter) is real. Only the imagined replies from "Michael" are fictional. The reader is invited to make "Michael" real by becoming Michael.

Above all, the issue is real. It's what the agnostic William James called a "live issue," like a live wire. It makes a difference. It makes a difference to everything. If God does not exist, then religion is the biggest hoax, the biggest myth, the biggest lie in the history of the world. If God does exist, then religion (which means "binding relationship") is the biggest truth, the biggest relationship in life: the relationship with the creator and designer of our existence, our identity, and our end. Every honest person must demand to know which is the truth, atheism or theism. For there is only one honest reason why anybody should ever believe anything: because it is true. And there is only one honest reason why anybody should ever disbelieve anything: because it is not true.

Reason, reasoning, arguing, dialectic, logic, dialogue, conversation—all seven of these English words are translations of the Greek word *logos*—is one way of finding truth. It is a distinctively human way; animals can't do it. We can.

So let's begin.

1

Dear Michael,

You don't know me (yet), and I don't know you (yet), but I met your sister Martha in Baltimore last week at a religious conference where I was speaking—what a marvelously mature and motherly woman she is for a single twenty-something!—and you came up indirectly in our conversation. We were talking about how good and wise some atheists are, and she mentioned you. She asked me whether I knew any good books to explain religious faith to such atheists, and I couldn't come up with one that I thought satisfactory. (She said you already read C. S. Lewis's *Mere Christianity* a long time ago.) She obviously both loves and respects you very much and hopes you can at least come to understand and even respect and sympathize with her faith, even though you don't believe it. And, of course, she wishes you could share it. But, she said, "I don't want to bash his brains with a Bible."

That's her motive. What's mine? This letter of mine to you, and any subsequent letters that I may come to write if you agree to be in a friendly debate with a theist, is motivated first of all by the fact that I'd like to be your friend, and I'd also like to help you and Martha to be better friends—because I believe that friendship

3

is a self-evidently good and precious thing. You certainly don't have to believe in God to believe in friendship.

Of course I'll argue with you, if you let me, and you with me: we will give what we think are the best reasons for believing the different things we believe. But behind this is a "heavier" motive: love. Friendship is, after all, a form of love. And also the desire for better understanding—understanding both of these two ideas (atheism and theism) and also of these two persons (you and me).

If you believe that atheism is true and that God is therefore a superstition, a kind of Santa Claus for grown-ups, then I assume that out of love and friendship you would want to persuade us believers out of our childish superstition, if possible, because you care about us and our intellectual maturity. I hope you will agree with the saying of St. Thomas Aquinas that "there is no greater act of charity to a friend than to lead him to the truth"—*whatever* that truth may be.

In other words, I'm assuming that you are both (1) honest and (2) loving. If you're honest, you must agree that the only honest reason to believe anything, whether atheism or theism, is that it's true. And if you love your friends, you must hope they becomes as enlightened about the truth as you are. So your motive for accepting this offer to debate with me by letter, as Martha's stand-in, so to speak, is the same as mine: we both love and respect Martha as we both love and respect truth. I think that's a great starting point for a debate: we are in deep agreement about two absolute, inherent, self-evident values, truth and love, even though we are in deep disagreement about whether God exists or not.

If we can both say a hearty yes to that, I think we can have a profitable exchange of friendly letters. What do you say?

Your friend (I hope),

Peter

2

Dear Michael,

Your acceptance of my proposal of friendship and dialogue made me very happy because it spoke a hearty yes to two deep desires of every human heart: (1) to understand and be understood, and (2) to love and be loved, in at least some of their many forms, for example, (1) logical argument and (2) friendship.

You probably know stories of people who claim to have had near-death experiences or out-of-body experiences. Many of these people, from a great diversity of religious or nonreligious backgrounds, say that they met a "being of light," which of course religious believers identify as God. If you are right in your atheism, this—and other religious experiences too—is explained, in a kind of Freudian way, as wishful thinking, for these people all say the same two things about this "being of light": that it (or He) *understood* them perfectly and *loved* them unreservedly. That is exactly what you would expect if we created God in our own image rather than vice versa, but also if God created us in His image. For these are the two deepest desires of the human heart, the two things that make us the most truly and deeply happy: to be known and to be loved.

Where am I going with this? Bear with me for a little while longer. It is difficult, if not impossible, for us to do both of these things to each other perfectly and totally. For when we know others' faults, we know how unlovable they are. Sartre is quite profound about this in his play *No Exit*. (Have you read it?) So you atheists have a strong argument against those who use such experiences of the "being of light" (or, for that matter, other religious experiences) as arguments for God's existence, since the experience, remarkable as it is, can be explained in these two opposite ways. The key could be designed to fit the lock or the lock designed to fit the key. It's either wishful thinking, "too good to be true," or it's so good *because* it's so true. Either the match between heaven and earth was made on earth or it was made in Heaven.

So why do I bring up this issue if I think it proves nothing either way? To elicit your agreement that, whether there is God or no God, there is understanding and there is love, and these are two self-evidently good things, and that is the most basic basis of our writing these letters to each other.

Of course, we believe importantly different things about them: do they come down to us from Heaven or do they just come up from us, from earth, and invent a Heaven in their own image? But this difference, great as it is, can't negate our agreement about these two values. They are our *data*, and our opposite explanations of them (and of all other data, ultimately) are like two opposite hypotheses in science. (Of course, religion is not just a "hypothesis," but it is not less, I think; so the scientific analogy holds.) We cannot disagree about our different explanations unless we agree about our data.

3

Dear Michael,

I appreciate your reservation. You say, "What you say about understanding and love is surely right in theory, but in practice I think we will be motivated more by our desire to win the argument and change the other person's mind than by the unprejudiced search for truth." From the little I know of my own heart, I cannot wholly disagree with you. I agree that our motives are almost always mixed.

However, I do not see how we could draw a quantitative line and say that one motive contributes "more" than the other. (How much more? Over 50 percent? Of what?) But in any case this does not invalidate or imperil our dialogue, I think, (1) because we are both aware of it and (2) because we both want to overcome it, to be totally honest and objective, however difficult that may be, and (3) because we are both in the very same leaky boat here. We start equal.

You wrote that you think you are "much more skeptical, more of a skeptical kind of *person*" than I am. Perhaps so, perhaps not. But even if so, this does not make profitable dialogue impossible. If anything, it makes it more likely, for everything is tested and honed by its opposite, by challenge.

Imagine two scientists. One is skeptical in temperament and also skeptical about whether there is any Loch Ness Monster. The other is less skeptical both in temperament and about the monster. So what? As long as both accept the same logical rules, the same scientific method, and the same data, they can argue fruitfully and perhaps discover the truth. Why can't two philosophers do the same?

(And don't say you are not a philosopher. Everyone is a philosopher, and those of us who do philosophy professionally, like myself, are not necessarily better philosophers than others. Perhaps the "amateurs" are the true lovers and we "professionals" are intellectual prostitutes. That's what Socrates would say.)

If, on the other hand, you don't believe there is any such thing as objective truth, then we can't argue about God or anything else until we settle that preliminary issue. But I think you couldn't be a successful working scientist, as you are, if you didn't believe in the existence and knowability of objective truth, could you?

Perhaps there are a few exceptions to that rule. I once met a man who believed in the religion of Mary Baker Eddy, the founder of "Christian Science" (which is neither Christian nor science). Christian Scientists believe that the whole material universe is an illusion, a dream, a projection of "spirit"; that matter does not exist. Matter is subjective, and thus all truth about matter is subjective. This man actually taught physical chemistry at a prestigious Little Ivy League college. I asked him how he could do that without hypocrisy, and he answered, cheerfully, "Oh, I just tell my students that I personally believe that matter is not objectively real at all, but that this illusion has wonderfully consistent properties, which we shall study in this course."

Well, if I believed what he believed, I wouldn't think it worthwhile to spend time either teaching or learning about the "wonderfully consistent properties" of this "illusion." I suspect you wouldn't either. So I hope you do believe that it's objectively true, in fact, that there is no God. Because if you only believe that God is not "true for you" but may be "true for me," I must confess I have never been able to figure out what that could possibly mean, even though many people say such things. If truth is "for me" or "for you," what is the difference between truth and illusion, truth and error, truth and falsehood?

How tedious you find it when someone tells you all about the dream he had last night! (Unless you are a psychiatrist.) So if all we're going to do in these letters is tell each other about our own private dreams of atheism and theism, I don't see how it would not be as tedious as a long, long dream talk.

Are you with me so far? If so, can we get into the interesting questions now?

Your friend,

Peter

4

Dear Michael,

No, I'm not impatient and disappointed that you want "to be sure our starting point and motives are right before we begin." I quite agree that "impatience and haste is the cause of most of the mistakes most of us make in most areas of life, from science to driving a car."

You demand of me more clarification of what I mean by "the motive of seeking the truth whatever it might be." I appreciate that demand and the fact that you call it a "demand," not just an "ideal," and I shall try to meet that demand. You call yourself a "troublemaker" for that, apologetically; but I think you should not be apologetic at all, because philosophers need that kind of "troublemaker." That's why I'd want to include at least one tough-minded, "troublemaking" Socrates or G. E. Moore–type philosopher in every philosophy department.

What I mean by the motive of truth seeking is more than a mere "motive." It has to be a *passion*. It has to be unqualified, or "fanatical." If you own a copy of Pascal's *Pensées*, read the section "Against Indifference" and perhaps also the section on "Diversion." You don't have to like his famous "wager" to appreciate those two sections. And, to anticipate your question, I don't plan to use his "wager" as an argument for God, because it doesn't mean to *prove* that God exists at all.

(Pascal's "wager," in case you don't know it, is not an attempt to prove that God exists, but that it's reasonable to "bet" that He does because if you lose, you lose nothing, and if you win, you gain everything (Heaven). Actually, Pascal's version is much less crude and more subtle than that summary, and I'd recommend reading his *Pensées* in any case as a literary masterpiece, even if you find its arguments less than convincing.)

Perhaps I can make my point about the passion for objective truth clear by making it radical. You have given your life to science, as I have given my life to philosophy. We both have given up our lives to the search for truth, in different though related fields. I am arguing with you about atheism for a number of reasons: (1) first of all, for the sake of truth, for the sake of our both coming to discover more truth, whatever and wherever it is, because that's always good for everybody involved, (2) and for friendship, both with you and with Martha, (3) and for delight and profit for me, and (4) for delight and profit for you. This last point refers both to the delight in the process of arguing and also to the delight in the truth at the end of the process, if it succeeds.

And of course I hope that I may be able to persuade you about God. Why else would one argue, except to persuade the other to accept something one already believes to be true?

On this last point, I think that science itself may save you, may convert you, may bring you to God. I don't mean any particular scientific argument, like the big bang or the anthropic principle (though that's possible too, and it has happened to a number of scientists and philosophers, like Antony Flew). I mean the essence of science, the essence of the scientific method, which is the total, passionate, open-minded, unprejudiced search for objective truth, whatever it is and wherever it is. I mean the tough-mindedness, the "will to truth" that Nietzsche sneered at, the nonnegotiable demand on yourself to follow the evidence and the argument wherever it leads.

If the God I believe in really exists—the God of the Bible, the God of Christianity—then He will honor that search for truth. "All who seek, find," Christ promised. He did not promise how long it would take (God's a lover, not an airline) or how twisted and obscure the path would be, but he promised that nothing could keep you from finding what you want if what you want is truth, truth with a capital *T*, ultimate truth, truth about God.

I think the only thing that can keep a seeker from finding it in the end is pride. I mean not just vanity but "my will be done" instead of "truth be done," the will to my own comfort or convenience or prestige or ease or autonomy or anything else at the expense of truth.

Even freedom. For true freedom comes only from truth: lies always enslave you. "The truth will make you free." And freedom is not just *from* truth but also *for* truth, not just for itself. Chesterton says an open mind is essential for the same reason an open mouth is essential: so that it can chomp shut on something solid to eat. So freedom is for truth as well as from truth. It's subordinate to truth.

So if you reject God and embrace atheism because you sincerely believe God is not true and atheism is, then you do not reject God, for God is truth.

Truth, after all, isn't just an abstract logical relationship between an idea or a proposition and the objective world. It's a

reality, something like light; something good and great and valuable and beautiful. Even when it's the truth about something ugly,
the fact that it's true is in itself something beautiful, like an honest
confession of murder in court. Truth is our right relation with
reality, whatever reality is. That's what Jesus promises you will get
if you seek it: the true relationship, the right relationship, with
reality. And if God is the ultimate reality, then it means God, in
the end.

If you agree about this, about truth, even though not about
God, then I think we are much closer together, at the center, than
most people think, both theists and atheists. And there is another
surprising way I suspect we may find out that we are together, and
that's about the idea we disagree about, the idea of God, at least
about what it means, even though not about whether it is true. To
find out whether my suspicion is correct, let me ask you a question: Do you *wish* there was a God? Not a cosmic dictator but a
loving father, I mean. And there is a second question: How do
you understand the meaning of the "God" you do not believe
exists? What do you think I believe when I say I believe in God?
Perhaps the God you deny is one I deny too.

These are the two questions I think we could profitably ask
each other if we want to clarify our starting points. And the two
are connected. For if you say no to the first (if you don't even *wish*
there was a God), then I think your answer to the second is also
different from mine; that is, I think you mean something by
"God" that is very different from what I (and other Christians)
mean by "God." For I think it is as impossible to wish we had no
heavenly father as it is to wish we had no earthly father. More so,
in fact. For only a very bad earthly father or a very bad relationship
with him could ever make anyone wish that he didn't exist. And

5

Dear Michael,

My two happy suspicions are fulfilled: you do "worship truth, though not God," as I hoped; and you *do* understand what "God" means. Good! You go even farther than I when you say "Only an arrogant, envious egotist would *resent* the existence of a perfect heavenly father that was other than and superior to himself." And then you go on to say: "I am convinced that the God idea is not too bad to be true but too good to be true, not too imperfect to be true, but too perfect to be true. It is indeed Santa Claus for so-called grown-ups."

But when you list the attributes of "God" you concentrate on "(1) total power, (2) total knowledge, and (3) total goodness." This is fine, but you then define "total goodness" as "being as good as it is possible to be." Which is also fine, but then you define "good" merely as "ontological perfection" and do not mention *moral* perfection, goodwill, charity, or love. Why? Is your concept of God the God of Aristotle and deism, a God who does not love us, rather than the God of Judaism and Christianity, who does? Or do you agree with me that the most important kind of perfection (or goodness) is moral perfection, and that love is the most essential ingredient in that?

Do you agree that whether or not there is a God, love is clearly life's highest value, that love is "the meaning of life"?

If so, the next question is: How real is love? Is it "bigger than both of us," to use the profoundly mystical old Hollywood cliché? Is it greater than us, so that we are in it rather than it being only in us? Is it like truth? Truth is not only in us (the silly idea of "my truth," or "subjective truth"); might not love also be not only in us?

You see where I'm going with this: Does love "go all the way up"? Is it the nature of ultimate reality? Does it "move the sun and all the stars," as Dante said? Is gravity "love among the particles"?

If you say yes to that, then it's only one short step to affirming a God of love—that is, affirming that the *best* thing (love) and the most *real* thing (God, ultimate reality) are one.

What I'm doing is not proving anything but setting up two opposite worldviews to choose between. And this setup is not arbitrary because it's based on the premise that all our experience has two poles, the subject and the object, the experiencer and the experienced, ourselves and objective reality. And at the heart of the subject pole of this universal duality, at the heart of the self, is—well, the heart. Where love comes from. The question, then, is whether at the heart of the object pole of this universal duality there is love too. If so, we fit reality, heart to heart, center to center. If not, not.

So my question to you now is this: (1) Do you agree with the above analysis, the two ultimate worldview options? Do you see the difference between atheism and theism as the difference between these two options? (2) If not, why not? And if so, why do you still see the reasons for atheism as stronger than the reasons for theism?

You can easily see *why* we theists choose the other option, I hope. Or do you think that it's no good reason at all, and nothing but wishful thinking? Do you not sense the claim of love to be "bigger than both of us" and a clue to what is most real? If you do sense this claim, what do you as an atheist do with it? If it's only your subjective desire, why does it have such authority?

Your friend,

Peter

6

Dear Michael,

Thank you for your very clear answer to my question. Can we separate it into two parts and discuss them separately? I think we must, because the two are so different that they almost contradict each other. One is your metaphysical nihilism, or "the nothingness of metaphysics," "the impossibility of any transcendent metanarrative or 'worldview' of 'the nature of reality' or 'the meaning of human life' as a whole," as you put it. The other point, which seems to be playing the very metaphysical game you disavow in your first point, is the credentials of your alternative worldview, your reasons for choosing atheism rather than theism.

Assuming that this is a good way to organize our discussion, I propose these three questions, in order: (1) Can we have good reasons for any "worldview" or metaphysics? If not, how can we even have this debate? (2) What are your reasons for atheism? (3) What are your reasons against theism? If you accept that agenda, let's begin with (1); if not, just ignore the rest of this letter and tell me why you think a different agenda is better.

Before we begin, let me emphasize that I was *not* putting forth my argument about love "going all the way up" as a "*proof* for the existence of God," only as a *clue* or a kind of road map of the two opposite roads. It's not a "proof" because it's not a deductive demonstration of a theistic conclusion from premises I expected you to accept. It's also not a "proof *of God*" because it doesn't prove, or even define a road to, a "God" already known and defined by a religion. I don't think any argument can prove all that a Christian or a religious Jew or a Muslim means by "God," only a very thin slice of that. In this case, the "slice" that this "argument" from love (insofar as it is an "argument" at all) is a clue to, or a road to, or leads to, is just *some* real presence of love at the heart or summit of reality, some basic match between our deepest aspiration and objective reality's deepest dimension. That's much more vague than "God." Do you deny even that first step, the movement from our experience of the supreme value of love to its ontological status, or do you deny the next step, the movement from that point (the ontological status of love) to God, to even a thin slice of God?

I hope you don't demand I define what I mean by "deepest" because that would probably get us into many technical arguments about meaning and verification and epistemology that would interest only philosophers. I think you know what I mean intuitively; that's why you call it "the biggest example of wishful thinking that has ever existed." So you do understand how "big" it is, how "wishful" it is. Since I don't know where we can profitably go from here about this particular issue, or argument, or whatever it is, let's just leave it hanging out to dry there, as a big sign at the crossroads, a double sign. Your part of it says "World's Biggest Fairy Tale," and mine says "World's Biggest Good News."

7

Dear Michael,

Just as I thought, we mean two very different things by "metaphysics."

I mean simply "thinking about being," asking questions about existence and essence and causality and other such universals. For instance, "Is all being good, or is some evil?" And "Can effects exceed their causes?" And "Is any being necessary, or are all contingent?"

You, on the other hand, mean by "metaphysics," according to your own description of it, "a super-science, a 'science of everything' that transcends all possible sense observation, mathematical measurement, or reduction to logical tautologies as ways of verifying or falsifying its statements."

I think our difference about metaphysics stems from our different starting points in epistemology. I start with the questions people naturally ask, in many different times, places, and cultures. You think these questions are unanswerable and fruitless because you begin with science as it has developed in one particular time, place, and culture: Europe and America in the last few centuries.

I have no quarrel with your starting point, but I think you have a quarrel with mine. For I accept the authority of science, though not the philosophical claim that nothing outside science has any kind of authority. I wonder whether you grant at least a probable or provisional or possible authority to common sense, or the human tradition, or the questions we ask naturally and intuitively. Do you not feel a *difficulty*, at least, in the fact that only a very small minority of all human beings who have ever lived have shared your metaphysical nihilism or metaphysical skepticism?

And do you feel a difficulty in the fact that so few have been atheists? Do you grant no authority to what Chesterton called "the democracy of the dead"? Do you grant no vote to those who have been disenfranchised not by accident of birth but by accident of death? To put it bluntly, how can you be an atheist without being a snob, at least a chronological snob? After all, if there is no God, almost all our ancestors have guided their lives most centrally, most ultimately, by an illusion. No, worse than an illusion, a collective insanity—that's how Freud describes all religion in *Civilization and Its Discontents*. It's even crazier than Jimmy Stewart's belief in Harvey, the giant invisible rabbit who is his best friend but which nobody else can see, in the old movie by that name. God is even bigger and more important than Harvey.

So I leave you with these three questions: (1) Do you deny all metaphysics, even in my sense of the word rather than yours? (2) If so, why? (3) And why don't you have to be a snob to be an atheist?

Your friend,

Peter

8

Dear Michael,

On the issue of "snobbery," I didn't mean to or want to get into the psychological issue, and I certainly didn't mean to imply that all atheists are in fact snobs or that you are. In fact, it's almost the exact opposite: only because I assumed that you *reject* snobbery do I think you have a *logical* problem being an atheist, since atheism *seems* to logically entail a "chronological snobbery." I was expecting you to show me why that did not logically follow.

But perhaps you did just that when you said that "truth is not found by voting." And I certainly agree with that. But don't you still have to share Freud's severe judgment of insanity on 95 percent or more of all human beings who have ever lived, the 95 percent who have been religious? And isn't that snobbish?

The more philosophical issue is metaphysics. I think you are right when you say that there is "no soft middle ground between us," between your view, which I call "scient*ism*," and mine, which you call "groundless superstition." Either the human mind can make rational judgments that are neither (1) empirical, nor (2) mathematical, nor (3) tautological, or it cannot. I say it can; you say that it cannot.

Let's first be sure we know exactly what we mean before we argue for our opposite answers. We agree that metaphysics is not empirical, but I say it begins with empirical data and checks its hypotheses by how well that data is explained. For instance, our empirical experience of plurality, change, and causality cannot be adequately explained by, and therefore refutes, the metaphysical monism or pantheism of Parmenides. I agree with Aristotle that all our knowledge begins with sensation ("soft empiricism"), but it does not end with it, and it is not limited to it: that's "hard empiricism." I do not defend the opposite epistemology or metaphysics, a Platonic, Cartesian, or Hegelian rationalism.

Similarly, I say that metaphysics—once we have data from experience—can be argued by formal logic, which is ultimately based on the law of noncontradiction; and this means showing that your opponent's false hypothesis entails a self-contradiction and therefore that the alternative hypothesis is or logically implies a tautology. For that's true of all logical argument about anything, not just metaphysics. For instance, take the old saw, "All men are mortal, and Socrates is a man; therefore, Socrates is mortal." We can show the validity of this argument by reducing the alternative to its conclusion to a self-contradiction. For if we accept the alternative of this conclusion, namely, that Socrates is *not* mortal, and also accept either one of the two premises of this syllogism, we contradict the other premise. For example, if Socrates is not mortal and all men are mortal, then Socrates is not a man. And if Socrates is not mortal and Socrates is a man, then not all men are mortal.

This logic is relevant to our discussion about whether metaphysical arguments for (or against) God are possible because the "Socrates is mortal" argument above is similar in its logic to many of the most famous arguments for God, for example, the design argument: whatever is full of design comes from a preexisting mind; nature is full of design; therefore, nature comes from a pre-existing mind. Whether this proves God or not, it's a legitimate *kind* of argument, and its premises do not fit into your three categories.

Since there are so many apparently good philosophical arguments for so many things that have premises that are not directly empirical, or mathematical, or tautological, it seems reasonable to me to demand from you some very good reasons for so severely restricting human knowledge to these three things only. It seems arbitrary, as if it were from the beginning designed to exclude metaphysics—and/or God.

Would you go as far as Hume did and say that even a metaphysical proposition as commonsensical as the principle of causality or the principle of sufficient reason—that whatever exists has a sufficient reason why it exists rather than not, or that whatever begins to exist has a cause for its beginning to exist—would you say, like Hume, that all such metaphysical principles are "nothing but sophistry and illusion"? Don't you have to presuppose this principle in science as much as I do in philosophy?

Your friend,

Peter

9

Dear Michael,

Yes, I guess I am asking you whether you are a logical positivist. That is, do you limit all meaningful propositions to tautological, mathematical, or scientific, empirically testable ones? Because that's what you seemed to say when you said that all legitimate judgments had to fit into your three classes. Actually, the logical positivists limited it to two classes, since they identified two of yours: mathematical propositions like $2 + 2 = 4$ and logical tautologies like $X = X$. As you probably know, they said that a proposition is meaningless if it is not verifiable in principle and then went on to limit verification to these two classes, empirical verification and purely logical (i.e., tautological) verification. Thus, propositions like "God exists" or "God does not exist" are neither true nor false but literally meaningless. And if you did say that you were a logical positivist, I would have asked you how you escape the obvious argument that this principle contradicts itself, eliminates itself, since it itself is neither empirical nor mathematical or tautological.

But you are aware of that difficulty, I see, and you reject "the absolute and exceptionless rule" or logical positivism's "verification principle." So that is not your reason for rejecting metaphysics. I didn't *think* you were that blind.

You say that your reason for rejecting metaphysics is "not a closed-minded, dogmatic, and arbitrary assumption like the verification principle but an open-minded 'show me' skepticism." Okay, then: tell me what's wrong with the examples of metaphysical principles I gave you in my last letter, like the principle of causality, and the metaphysical arguments that are based on them, like the causal arguments for a God or uncaused cause.

Until you answer that question, I don't think I should add any more arguments, even though that will make this letter very short.

Your friend,
Peter

10

Dear Michael,

You're right to probe into what is in the back of my mind, where I am "really headed" with this abstract talk about kinds of propositions and how metaphysical propositions can be meaningful. It is indeed more than my probe into the logic of propositions; it's my probe into what kind of atheism you hold. I would distinguish four kinds.

The most usual kind is an atheism that is also naturalistic, scientistic, and materialistic. That is, it does not admit the existence of anything supernatural, or superscientific, or supermaterial. So it's four claims: atheism, naturalism, scientism, and materialism.

A second kind, of which "secular humanism" is the most usual version, rejects materialism—it does not believe everything real is material—but it embraces scientism and naturalism as well as atheism.

A third kind rejects scientism as well as materialism but embraces naturalism as well as atheism. Buddhism is the most famous example of this. It can admit souls, spirits, minds, or selves (though Buddhism does not), and duties, and beauties, and real values, and other things that transcend both matter and science;

30

but it claims that there is nothing "outside" or in addition to the universe, the self-contained system or continuum of causes and effects, psychic as well as somatic, that we call nature.

A fourth kind rejects even naturalism and embraces something like Platonic ideas (Kai Nielson holds this) or G. E. Moore's "non-natural properties," such as "the good," but does not embrace God.

I think there is a natural gravity that draws the atheist to naturalism, then scientism, then materialism, but that this draw can be resisted. So what I'm "probing" for is whether I only have to argue against atheism or also against naturalism, scientism, and materialism. Which of these four is your premise for atheism? Because if nothing immaterial is real, nothing superscientific or supernatural can be real either; and if nothing superscientific is real, nothing supernatural can be either; and if nothing supernatural is real, God can't be real either.

Oh, by the way, I quite agree with you that arguing any more about syllogisms and tautologies and verification would be too technical to interest anyone but a philosopher, and I am happy to be redirected by you to more substantive and interesting aspects of our dialog. Which we haven't really gotten to yet, have we? We're still setting the agenda. Oh well, "well begun is half done," as some ancient Greek said. (I don't know whether it rhymed in Greek or not.)

Your friend,
Peter

11

Dear Michael,

You classify your answer to my questioning which of my four classes of atheism you fit into as "confused," but I'd classify it as both humble and ambitious: humble in confessing that you're not sure just which of the four classes of atheists you fit into and ambitious in wanting to find out. So you want to argue all four issues. Okay, here we go.

That habit that you say you learned from Martha, the instinct to try a "both/and" answer to any "either/or" question—I think that's a very healthy instinct just about everywhere. In fact, the only place "both/and" can't possibly work is mutually contradictory propositions. And even there, when we distinguish two or more possible meanings of one or more terms of one or both of the propositions, we often find that they only *seemed* to be mutually contradictory propositions.

By the way, I too personally "relate to" all four of the examples of "both/and" that you quoted from Martha: lying on the beach/swimming in the sea, summer/winter, childhood/maturity, and "hot" colors/"cool" colors. Especially the first one. Beach season is short and precious here in New England. But glorious. You should visit sometime.

Perhaps even atheism versus theism is an example of this principle that an apparent either/or can really be a both/and. For I suspect that the God you insist does not exist is probably a God I also insist does not exist; and perhaps the God I maintain does exist is a God you never denied.

For my concept of God is the being that is not only "that than which nothing greater can be conceived" but also "the being that is greater than *can* be conceived." Both parts of that description are from St. Anselm, who then goes on to use it in his famous "ontological argument." I think that his definition is good even though his "ontological argument" is fallacious.

So do you think we should discuss the four issues I defined together or one at a time? They are distinct but closely related. And if one at a time, for the sake of clarity, in what order? And if in what seems to be the most logical order—first materialism, then scientism, then naturalism, then atheism—how do we avoid the morass of getting stuck in three more too-long, too-abstract preliminary issues and not getting to the interesting and important one (God) until we're half dead? (Am I doing just that already?)

If you want a provisional proposal from me, how about a both/and here too? We begin with one letter each (no more) on materialism, scientism, and naturalism. Then we hit the God question straight on. That way we won't skip the logical preliminaries but we also won't linger on them.

Your friend,

Peter

12

Dear Michael,

Thanks for the personal compliment; I too look forward each day to getting another letter from you, and for the same two reasons you do: the clarity and the fairness of my dialog partner. And his evident goodwill.

Agreeing about our agenda, then, we begin with materialism. You say your "reason for believing it is, in a word, Science." (How interesting that you capitalize the *S* in Science but not the *G* in God! Is that a deliberate "in your face" ideological statement, like changing "BC and AD" to "BCE and CE"?) I too can put my reason for *not* believing materialism into one word: experience.

You say "Science observes no 'spirits,' and therefore knows no 'spirits,' since Science bases all knowledge on observation." But the mathematical sciences are surely legitimate sciences, yet they do not base *anything* on observation. And if you reply that mathematical entities, from simple positive integers to complex hypotheses like the mathematics of general relativity, are only *ideas* rather than real entities in the universe like quarks or quasars, then you have transcended materialism and also naturalism: you have gone beyond the physical universe. For mathematical ideas are not our subjective opinions; they are the objective truths that those subjective opinions opine. Four *really is* two plus two.

Experience surely does not lead to materialism. Don't you *experience* the difference between your mind and your body? Your *thought* of pain is not pain. The same needle, and the same physical pain it causes, can elicit opposite thoughts in different people: "It's my friend and it's only a needle" or "It's my enemy and it's killing me." Even emotionally, "I hate that" and "I accept that" are mentally different responses to the same pain. Thoughts and feelings are not the same as physical pains or pleasures.

The mental act, or mental energy, even of physical sensation, is not itself a physical thing. It has no size, shape, mass, or color. It has mental energy but not kinetic energy.

Here's a simple logical argument against materialism. Premise one: the knowledge *of* a thing is not one of that thing's parts or attributes. For example, the knowledge of a tree is not a root or a leaf. The knowledge of a thing is more than the thing; it transcends the thing known. Premise two: but we can know some truths about *everything* material (e.g., E equals MC squared). Conclusion: therefore, the knowledge of matter must be more than matter. Corollary: but knowledge of matter exists; therefore, not all that exists is material.

To put it even more simply, materialism is an *ism*, not an atom. The very word contradicts itself.

That seems simply obvious and commonsensical to me, and not at all "spooky."

I think I understand your suspicion of what I call common sense. You think common sense, or at least traditional common sense, believes in "spirits all over the place, the Holy Spirit in Heaven and a little spirit pulling the strings of my brain and body, and spooky spiritual forces like 'purposes' and 'intelligent designs' haunting every blade of grass in the world." But surely when you read Plato or Aristotle you see that that's not what their antimaterialism means. They don't claim to see ghosts. They just claim they have minds as well as bodies and that things have form as well as matter: form not just in the sense of visible shape but inner identity, nature, essence. Every artist knows that the "form" of a statue is not the outside of the statue but the inside of the statue, as Chesterton says.

How does a materialist account for the stubborn fact of consciousness? If it's nothing but physical brain activity, then what is my consciousness *of* my physical brain activity? Remember, the *knowledge of* a thing cannot be one of the parts of the thing known. That can be proved by formal logic alone. For the alternative would make accurate knowledge (knowledge that matches the thing known) impossible. For in the very act of knowing all the facts about a thing you create a new fact about that thing: that it was known. And that fact can be known only by still another act of knowing, et cetera ad infinitum.

You see, I'm finding it hard to *argue* (arguing is what Aristotelian logic calls the "third act of the mind") when I suspect you don't really *understand* (understanding is what Aristotelian logic calls the "first act of the mind") what I and 99 percent of all human beings who ever lived on this planet *mean* by mind, thought, spirit, self, or soul.

Consciousness, after all, (1) cannot be denied to exist without self-contradiction (that's Descartes's point in "I think, therefore I am"), but (2) it has none of the properties that characterize everything that is material (size, shape, mass, etc.), and (3) it has properties that are not material (e.g., "truth"). The existence of consciousness seems to immediately refute materialism.

If your answer is the compromise of epiphenomenalism, which grants some reality to the immaterial but claims that it is adequately explained by merely material *causes*, then you are still denying the immediate experience we all have of the causal relationship working the other way: I move my arm and tongue *because* I first think and will to do so.

Another argument against epiphenomenalism is that if thought is a mere by-product of matter, a kind of fart of the brain, then you can't account for the *validity* of thought—of any thought, and therefore of that thought too. If we can't help how our tongues just happen to wag because some blind and dumb molecules are pushing it one way rather than another, then why should you pay attention to my words any more than to the tea leaves in the fortune-teller's cup? It seems to me that materialism is akin not to science but to primitive superstition.

Your friend,
Peter

13

Dear Michael,

You are very gracious and honest in admitting that you "have never given careful attention to these difficult philosophical questions," and very practical in wanting "to move on to the rest of our agenda without taking a long course in the philosophy of mind." And no, I don't think that's a dishonest cop-out because you honestly confess that you *may* be wrong about this "ism" (materialism).

So let's look at scientism.

I do *not* define it as "the idolizing of science" (though I may have written that somewhere). That's a theological definition, not a logical one. I define it as the epistemological claim that science *and only science* can give us reliable, or verifiable, or trustworthy, or true, or useful, knowledge. (I do not say "certain" knowledge because most of the physical sciences, as distinct from the mathematical sciences, claim to give us only very probable knowledge most of the time. Correct me if I'm wrong about that; you know the sciences better than I do.)

Scientism seems to me to suffer from two fatal flaws. One is logical self-contradiction. For scientism is not a scientific claim about the universe but a philosophical claim, a claim in epistemology, about human knowledge, about the relation between human knowledge and science (or the scientific method). The claim is that *only* scientific knowledge, knowledge by the scientific method, is reliable. But that claim cannot be verified or falsified by the scientific method. There is no empirical data, no mathematical measurement, and no logical reduction of the opposite claim (that knowledge extends beyond science) to a self-contradiction. If all knowledge claims that cannot in principle be verified or falsified by the scientific method are unreliable and should be rejected, then that very statement is unreliable and should be rejected.

My other objection is even simpler. How can the reliability of *one* kind of knowledge (science) disprove the reliability of *other* kinds of knowledge? That's like the ear telling the eye that it is unreliable just because it can't hear anything, or like the mystic telling the scientist that he cannot have any valid knowledge of reality because he has never had a mystical experience.

How could science, which validly explores the physical universe and only the physical universe, possibly prove either that there is or that there is not something else real besides the physical universe? It has no data beyond scientific data. It can't, by its very nature. Saying there are no souls because "science sees no souls" is like saying there can be no souls because souls do not leave fossils or emit radiation. It's a really simple point: How could a fish whose experience is confined to its fishbowl know whether there's a world outside the fishbowl?

It might, perhaps, have some clues, like fingerprints, from which it could reason to an unseen finger as the cause of the seen fingerprint. So it might have relevant scientific data *for* the existence of something beyond its science (or it might not); but it certainly could not possibly have the opposite kind of data and evidence. How could there be data for something that does not exist?

The analogy of the fishbowl is imperfect because there can be something outside a fishbowl, but there can be nothing literally "outside" the universe, since space is not a Newtonian absolute but is relative to matter, and the universe is the sum total of all material things. And just as there is no space beyond the universe, as if it had a set of outside walls, similarly there is no time before the big bang, the beginning of all matter; no time before the beginning of time, since time is also relative to matter.

Many atheists define the universe as the sum total of all that exists rather than as the sum total of all material things. That begs the question in favor of materialism, assuming what it's trying to prove, identifying matter and real existence.

The point of my argument is logical, but there's a psychological side to it too. It seems insufferably arrogant, or at least childishly narrow-minded, to assume scient*ism* just because science itself works so well. It seems similar to a little kid discovering a new toy that makes him very happy and claiming that there could not possibly be any other toy that could make him happy too.

I'll wait to hear your answers to my critique of scientism before going on to argue about naturalism versus supernaturalism.

Your friend,

Peter

14

Dear Michael,

Okay, you make two strong points, one general, one specific. The general one is that the scientific method is the greatest discovery in the whole history of science (which I think is quite true), and that it makes you "tough-minded" rather than "tender-minded" (which is also true), and that compared to it, all other methods of thinking—ways of thinking that are symbolic or mystical or religious or instinctive—are "tender-minded" and therefore "inferior, though not worthless." Well, I can't quite agree with that. It softens your scientism but it does not abandon it. For though unscientific thought may be inferior by *scientific* standards, science itself can't prove whether or not there are other standards by which other kinds of thought might be superior.

Your second, more specific point is your reply to my two objections to scientism, namely, that it is self-contradictory and that it is arrogant or narrow-minded. You reply by putting the onus of proof on me when you say, "You grant me that the scientific method really does prove some objective truths reliably, but I do not grant you that any other method has ever done this. Can you prove to me that religion or philosophy or what you call common sense has ever done what I say Science alone can do?"

To your first point I reply that I am *not* "tender-minded" but as "tough-minded" as you are. I would define these two "minds" (notice how we have already escaped materialism!) not as scientistic versus nonscientistic or as materialistic versus nonmaterialistic but simply as "seeking objective truth first and foremost" versus "seeking something else (e.g., happiness or goodness) first and foremost." In other words, I define the difference between tough-mindedness and tender-mindedness in terms of the psychological starting point, in terms of motive, rather than in terms of their opposite *isms*, their controversial ideological conclusions or assumptions, their worldviews.

If we can define the two minds this way, I agree with your choice to be tough-minded. That's why I no longer believe in Santa Claus, even though when I was very young that belief made my feelings happier and my behavior better every December. Truth trumps everything. But that's the same reason I still believe in God, even when that belief is inconvenient: I believe in God for the only honest reason anyone should believe anything: because it's true, not because it's happifying or even goodifying or edifying.

In fact, I think that if God were to judge four people who died at the same time, (1) a tough-minded theist, (2) a tough-minded atheist, (3) a tender-minded theist, and (4) a tender-minded atheist, He would rank them in exactly that order. The tender-minded theist (number 3) would get a more severe purgatory than the tough-minded atheist (number 2) because he failed to learn lesson one, that truth trumps everything.

I'd classify Aquinas as a tough-minded theist, Camus as a tough-minded atheist, Kant as a tender-minded theist (because he said we must live "as if God existed" in order to live a fully moral life, even if God didn't exist), and Nietzsche as a tender-minded atheist. That last example may surprise you because Nietzsche sounds like a wild proto-Nazi and inveighs against tenderness. But he disbelieves in objective truth. He criticizes "the will to truth" and writes, "Why truth? Why not rather untruth?" He clearly confesses that the reason he is an atheist is that he couldn't stand having God know and judge his "dwarf," his "dark side." He writes: "I will now disprove the existence of all gods. If there were gods, how could I bear not to be a god? *Consequently,* there are no gods." In other words, he honestly confesses his dishonesty.

What I said earlier about both truth (or understanding, the understanding of truth) and love being absolutes and about the need that these two be united, not opposed, does not make me tender-minded, as you charged, because my reason for that conclusion is *not* that it makes me happy but because it is true. My ultimate reason is not even that God loves it, because I say God loves it because it is true, not that it is true because God loves it. I agree with Socrates against Euthyphro that a thing is not good just because God wills it but God wills it because it is good. God is no hypocrite in demanding that we be totally honest; He practices what He preaches. Anyone who believes in God but not in truth does not believe in the true God; and anyone, even an atheist, who disbelieves in God only because he believes in truth really believes in the true God. God is not "the boss"; God is the truth.

To your second point I say I must return to you the gift of the burden of proof. For if your scientism is right, then everyone in the world up until the discovery of the scientific method a few hundred years ago, including many of the great scientists as well as all the great philosophers, never once proved anything at all, because they didn't confine themselves to the modern scientific method. To say that is just "chronological snobbery." That is to take seriously David Hume's joke (I hope it was meant as a joke) in the last paragraph of his *Enquiry*: whatever is not empirical or mathematical deserves to be burned. Caliph Omar burned the books in the great library at Alexandria because they were not part of his Koran. Do you want to burn all the books that are not part of your new Koran of science? Do you want to burn Socrates, Plato, Aristotle, Aquinas, da Vinci, Confucius, Buddha, Lao Tzu, Muhammad, Aken-aton, all as "sophistry and illusion"? Was truth first discovered by Francis Bacon?

Isn't it more reasonable to be skeptically open-minded rather than dogmatically closed-minded and begin with the working assumption that any and all other ways to truth may well do the job until they are shown to fail? Why not begin, as Socrates did, by assuming his interlocutor was right until he found fallacies that proved him wrong? Why not be maximally open-minded? Are you on the side of Galileo or on the side of the bishops who refused to look through his telescope? Isn't the very first step of the scientific method to question all prejudices, to begin by opening your mind rather than closing it?

Forgive me for sailing so close to the wind of personal insult here. I do not mean to accuse you of closed-mindedness; in fact, everything you have written reveals the opposite mind-set to me. That is my whole point. I don't see how an open-minded person can embrace scientism or any other narrowing ism. Neither philosophy nor religion wants to murder science; why should science want to murder philosophy or religion?

Your friend,

Peter

15

Dear Michael,

Your long and detailed reply to my "passionate" letter raises many specific questions that I am happy to discuss later (Galileo, Darwin, the Inquisition, etc.). But I was not proposing an "Okay, tough guy, let's take off the puffy boxing gloves and go bareknuckle" approach. My main point is logical rather than psychological: that science cannot prove scientism.

I think Iunderstand your answer to my claim that there are other reliable methods of finding objective truth than science. It's basically: "I'm from Missouri. Show me. I'll believe it when I see it." But my obedience to your imperative "Show me!" would be to show you the whole history of human thought before this little enclave of it that contains modern science. Surely your education has not been that provincial? For instance, take any one of Socrates's dialogs. Are all his arguments fallacious or sophistic? Is logic itself worthless until integrated into the scientific method?

Should I pick one particular argument that I think really proves its conclusion but not by the scientific method so that we can argue about that particular example? I'm willing to do that if you insist, but I fear it would be a bit tedious and technical.

Atheism is so much more interesting than epistemology! I'm impatient to argue about it. Perhaps that's unphilosophical of me.

So this is a short "agenda" letter rather than a long "substantive argument" letter. If you agree, can we go on to talk about naturalism versus supernaturalism now? Or do you think we are copping out on unresolved issues regarding scientism? Or perhaps you want to skip the step about naturalism because there are so few atheists who could be classified as supernaturalists? Or do you think we should alter our agenda in some other way?

Your friend,

Peter

16

Dear Michael,

I'm pleased that you "want to talk more philosophy first before we go on to religion, but about the big questions instead of the little questions." What you say you want to explore is what is traditionally called the issue of faith and reason. You say that faith is not just false but irrational. So let's leave our previous topic and go there, even though if any professional philosophers read our letters they would be disappointed that we left so many issues in epistemology hanging out to dry. So what? They're dry to begin with. And we have the freedom to shine the little flashlights of our minds into any corner of the big, dark world that we want to.

(By the way, if you agree that we have that freedom, you believe in free will. But isn't free will incompatible with atheism? It's certainly incompatible with materialism and naturalism, because both of those philosophies imply determinism. Another question for another day.)

Before we can intelligently argue about whether "religious faith is irrational," we need to define "reason." I suspect that most of our misunderstandings of each other will stem from the different meanings we attach to this key term. What "reason" meant

47

before the scientific method and the Scientific Revolution, before Bacon's inductive scientific philosophy, before Descartes's deductive mathematical philosophy, and before Kant's "Copernican Revolution in philosophy," which claimed that reason cannot intuit or even discover but only calculate and create or shape the order that it knows—this earlier meaning of "reason," as exemplified by Socrates, is a much broader thing than the later one. We need to know which meaning we are using or we will pass each other like two warships in the fog, and no shots from either ship will land on the other one.

Let's distinguish five different questions, which involve four different things that "reason" or "rational knowledge" may be said to accomplish. If you disagree with this, please say so, because otherwise we will share misunderstood misunderstandings instead of understood misunderstandings. I think understood misunderstandings are the necessary middle step if we are to rise from misunderstood misunderstandings to mutual understandings.

1. A thing may *exist* without our reason *knowing* it. In other words, truth is objective.
2. We may *know* a thing without being *certain*. In other words, probable knowledge, or "right opinion," as Plato says, knows *something*.
3. We may be *certain* of something without a *proof* of it. In other words, not all certainty is deductive.
4. We may have a *proof* that is not a *scientific* proof. In other words, Socrates proved *some* things.

So we should distinguish (1) existence, (2) knowledge, (3) certainty, (4) proof, and (5) science.

Intelligent beings on other planets, or their absence, exists (1) though we don't know it (2). The goodwill and reliability of my pilot or surgeon is probable (2) but not certain (3). I trust, believe, and opine that he is not a terrorist spy. I'm certain (3) that I exist and have a headache, but I can't prove it to you (4). Even Descartes admitted that "I think, therefore I am" is certain only to the individual doing the thinking. And unless Socrates was a fool, not all proofs (4) use the scientific method (5).

Now let's apply these categories to religious faith in God.

All believers claim that God exists (1) *and* that we can know this (2). (To *say* that He exists is to claim to know it!)

No believers claim that God's existence can be proved by the scientific method (5).

Believers divide into three categories. Some believers claim that God's existence is only subjectively certain but that it cannot be objectively certain because it cannot proved objectively at all. They only go up to level (2). Some believe that there are objective arguments for Him but that they are only probable rather than certain. They go up to level (3). And some believe that there are some arguments that are certain. They go up to level (4).

I'm in that last category. I think there are some arguments that claim to prove that a being deserving the name "God" exists really do prove that, since they have no ambiguous terms, false premises, or logical fallacies. This is the classical, mainline position among Christians: Augustine, Aquinas, Newman, C. S. Lewis, and the Catholic Church say this.

Of course, the "God" such proofs prove is only a very thin slice of the God religious believers claim to know by faith in divine revelation (or, in the case of Hinduism, by mystical experience). It is more a deistic God than a theistic one: merely *some*

Unmoved Mover, Uncaused Cause, Necessary Being, Perfect Being, or Intelligent Designer. That's a far cry from the God of the Bible, but it's an even farther cry from atheism; and it does not *contradict* the God of the Bible, but it contradicts atheism.

Now for the relationship between faith and reason: If the faith is true, then it can never be contrary to reason. Since truth cannot contradict truth, no truths about God that reason cannot prove but can be known only by faith in divine revelation (if there are any such truths) can possibly contradict any truths about God that reason can prove. Only falsehoods contradict truths.

A corollary is that all arguments unbelievers bring against the content of religious faith, if it is, as it claims, divine revelation, have a false conclusion and therefore must have a false premise, or an ambiguous term, or a logical fallacy, and therefore can be answered by reason alone, not just by faith.

That is why I accept both the onus of proof and the onus of disproof, that is, the responsibility for refuting all objections. That's how confident I am that religious faith is rational. Not all of it can be proved by reason alone (e.g., the Trinity), but much of it can, and none of it can be disproved.

That's my fortress. Now knock it down. Prove it's a sand castle.

Your friend,
Peter

17

Dear Michael,

I'm surprised and pleased: surprised that you are surprised at my "rationalism" and pleased that you are pleased by it.

You ask me, "If religious faith is so rational, why are there so many intelligent atheists?" Part of the answer must be that there are also good reasons *against* God: for instance, the problem of evil, the apparent ability of the sciences to account for everything without God, and the bad behavior of believers. There are also good reasons *for* God, as I shall try to show. So there is plenty of "wiggle room."

Your next question surely will be: Why did God leave so much "wiggle room" when He could have shut the door to atheism by making all believers saints and performing miracles every day?

Because religion is a relationship. It's more like marriage than like science or math. Romeo does not propose to Juliet in syllogisms. He leaves her free to believe him or not, trust him or not, love him or not, elope with him or not. God does the same. Pascal says He gives us just enough light, just enough evidence, so that those who truly seek Him can find Him, but not so much that those who don't seek and don't care will find Him against their own will. He seduces our souls but does not rape them. He is a gentleman. So we all get what we want: we become single or married (to God). No shotgun weddings.

You seem to assume that because I am what you call a "rationalist" (I accept the label only in the Thomistic sense, not in the Cartesian sense; I would call myself an Aristotelian "soft empiricist"), I must therefore accept Clifford's rule: that it is always wrong (in fact, morally wrong) to believe anything beyond the evidence that proves it. No, I do not accept that. And neither do you, except when you are doing science. When a friend tells you, "It's raining," you don't reply, "Prove it!" or "I won't believe it till I see it." Clifford's rule is a real conversation stopper!

Did you ever read William James's famous essay "The Will to Believe"? It's a reasonable pragmatic alternative to and critique of Clifford. (James, by the way, was a lifelong agnostic.) C. S. Lewis's essay "On Obstinacy in Belief" says much the same thing a little more simply.

The legitimacy of Clifford's rule inside science and its illegitimacy outside science seem equally obvious to me. A basic rule of the scientific method is what Descartes called universal methodic doubt: every idea should be treated as guilty (false) till proven innocent (true). But people should be treated in the opposite way: as innocent till proven guilty. And religion is a blend of both, I think. It's a set of ideas to believe (or disbelieve) intellectually, but it's also a divine person to trust (or not to trust) personally. Belief in an idea is an opinion; belief in a person is a relationship.

Your friend,

Peter

18

Dear Michael,

Again you surprise me with your surprise. What I gave you is only the old, standard, traditional line about faith and reason. The fact that you find it "surprisingly intelligent" means that you have not, until now, been exposed to even the most basic philosophical foundations of the thing you call "the greatest fallacy and superstition in human history." That's not your fault; they never taught you. But it *is* a fault to attack a "straw man." It's a recognized logical fallacy. I'm not happy no one ever taught you that mainline, traditional religious believers claim their faith is rational, but I am happy you are open to correcting the "straw man" concept of faith *versus* reason that you had assumed.

When we examine a religious faith, we find it making claims on both head and heart, claims to be both true and good, or beautiful. Whatever the relation is between the head and the heart (and it's probably complex and largely subconscious), it's got to be equal in the sense that both have a veto power. A religion has to satisfy both. For if the heart sees a religious faith (or for that matter a secular philosophy or ideology) as evil and ugly and nasty and miserable and unlovable, then probably no arguments are going to convince that head. So if you see God as a picky, legalistic, puritanical tyrant, you're going to be suspicious a priori of even the most logical arguments for that God. Equally, if the head sees the faith as stupid and illogical, then no matter how happy and lovable it looks to the heart, the head will veto it—like Santa Claus—and instruct the heart to love it less. That's why I'm eager to correct your "straw man" misperceptions of my philosophy as irrational and "tender-minded." And I'm equally eager for you to correct any of my "straw man" misperceptions of yours.

That's also why I was happy you said you agreed with Freud's "wish fulfillment" explanation of faith. Why does that make me happy? Because if you think it's "too good to be true," you at least see how good it is. Your heart likes it even though your head vetoes it. When you see how beautiful the world is and how beautiful human love is, I suspect you at least *want* to believe that all this came not just from blind chance but from a loving creator and designer, don't you? So you wish it were true and maybe even hope it's true, but you don' t believe it's true. If the photo my mind is taking of your mind is crooked or foggy or skewered here, please correct me.

Martha called me last night to thank me for writing to you. I said to her that it felt strange to be *thanked* for accepting a gift: the gift of a new, interesting, and intelligent friend with whom to play the serious but delightful game of philosophical dialogue.

She loves you very deeply, you know. I hope you sense that, underneath her obvious religious concern that must make you feel a bit uncomfortable: I mean the "worried mother" role and the plea, "Doctor Kreeft, please fix my broken brother." (Of course, she never said that, but you naturally felt it.) I would be delighted, of course, if you ever discovered and embraced the joy and wisdom that Martha has from her religion, but I do not feel like a doctor trying to "fix" a patient. I feel like a friend who is privileged to know another friend who is like a piece of steel that my piece of flint can hit against to produce flashes of light for both of us, *whatever* the light may prove to illuminate.

You ask about how "personal" my faith is. I'm not sure whether you mean (1) whether I'm content to claim only that it is "personally true" or "true for me"—I think you must know the answer to that question already from our letters; or (2) whether you fear I'm arguing with you to "fix" you for Martha's sake (I think I just answered that question above); or (3) whether what you want to know is what personal, "existential" difference it makes to me that I believe what you do not. I suspect it is number 3.

That is a very good question. It shows how fair and open-minded you are. You want to know what it is that you don't believe; you don't want to refute a "straw man." Most of the famous and clever atheists in print today seem to lack that receptivity, that willingness to listen. Good listeners are much rarer than good talkers. As I want to listen to you, you want to listen to me. That's the fundamental prerequisite for any conversation or dialogue or argument that's honest and real and not just a "look how much cleverer I am than you are" performance.

So you want to know just what it is I believe. More than that, you want to know how it feels, what difference it makes to my life every moment. Good. Life is too short to waste on things that make no difference except in words, or in thoughts that don't *do* anything except sit there passively, like labels on unused drawers. That's another point of William James: the "pragmatic test" of an idea's truth, he says, is the difference it makes to our experience. I'd say that's the test of an idea's *meaning*, or meaningfulness rather than its *truth*, but with that correction I agree with it. And judging from your question to me, I think you do too.

So what difference does it make to me? Intellectually, it's *not* that it just adds one more ingredient at the top of my philosophy, like the capstone to an arch or the highest animal on a totem pole. It's more like the difference the sun makes. You can't look directly at it, as you can look at anything else; but it is the light, and the source of light, that lights up everything else in the universe and in your life. Literally. If, as Jesus says, it is true that not a single hair ever falls from our head, or not one sparrow ever falls from the sky, without the attention and permission and plan of God, then we can't see even one hair or one tiny, forgotten bird, in the same way again, ever. The whole *story* we're in is different.

Suppose you took every single literal, physical incident and character in *The Lord of the Rings* and retold the whole story not from the Catholic, mythic, epic, heroic mind-set and point of view of Tolkien, but from the nihilistic, pessimistic, antiheroic, skeptical, atheistic mind of Sartre or Beckett. It would be a totally different story. Every particular ingredient would be there, all the characters and events, but everything would mean something very different, ultimately, in the last analysis. It would be like reading *Hamlet* on the assumption that the ghost was an illusion and Hamlet was really insane.

You also ask me what difference it makes to me that I "believe the Christian religion rather than any of the many other alternatives to atheism." I have to give you two answers here, or two levels of answer.

First, Jesus is a Jew and completely accepts the Jewish claim about God (He claims to be the Son of *that God*), the claim that God is as He has revealed Himself to the Jews. He is a person rather than a force, as in "Star Wars" or Upanishadic Hinduism, or a mode of consciousness, as in Buddhism. He calls Himself *"I"*—"I AM." He has a character and a moral will. He loves: He loves goodness and not evil, and He loves all His creatures, especially us, even when we don't love Him. That's why He shouts and screams so much, just like a parent.

Second, according to Christianity, He loves us so much, even when we're wicked (because we need Him more then), that He comes to us and dies for us. (Don't ask me how that works; I don't even know how my TV set works.) He loves us—how much? That much, twelve-quarts-of-blood much.

The divine love is already in Judaism and also in Islam ("Allah the Compassionate, the Merciful"), though the incarnation is not. The very center of Christianity is Jesus, not merely as the greatest man who ever lived but God incarnate, literally. And the difference this makes is that He's not just past but present, not dead but alive. It's not just that "He rose" but that "He is risen." And He sent His spirit to inhabit us, to move us, to *haunt* us. Being a Christian is something like being a haunted house, but the ghost is the Holy Ghost. (The analogy is obviously wrong in many ways, but right in some, too.)

So either Christians are as insane as Jimmy Stewart in *Harvey*, or else this faith of ours is the supreme secret of sanity, of living in the real world. It is either the most colossal hoax in history, as you say, or the most fundamental meaning of life, just as Jesus himself is either the biggest liar in history ("Hi there, I'm God.") or the biggest nut case in history if he actually believed that lie, or else

He is What Absolutely Everything Is All About. The one and only thing he could not possibly be, logically, is the thing I'm pretty sure you believe he is: just a good man, a wise man. A priori, before you look at the historical evidence, that seems to be by far the most likely hypothesis and the most comfortable one: that he is just like each of the other billions of human beings in history, just a little better and wiser. But his claim to be God logically eliminates that hypothesis. A man who claims to be God is not a good man; he's either God or a bad man—bad morally if he lies or bad mentally if he sincerely believes it. So you have to pick one of the only two that remain, the two personally uncomfortable but logically possible hypotheses. You have to worship Him or lock him up in an asylum.

I've tried to answer your "personal" question at the same time as giving a reason for my answer, a classic logical argument used by the earliest Christian apologists. (It's called the "either God or a bad man" argument.) The personal consequence of believing the central claim of Christianity—that Jesus is God—is shocking. It's like an earthquake. It changes everything; it reorders your whole life. So I had to try to explain why it's not an illogical exaggeration but a logical alternative that has convinced many intelligent people.

There are two ways this can challenge atheism. One is by reasoning "upwards" to argue from Jesus to God—if Jesus is trustable, he is trustable about God too. So if Jesus is trustable, God exists. But the usual order is the reverse: first show that God is real and then that Jesus is God incarnate. That's a more logical order since if there is no God, Jesus can't be God. But some prefer the more concrete approach: meet him in the Gospels and decide whether he is trustable or insane. If he is trustable, he will reveal God; he will lead you to God.

The two ways that I've called the "up" way and the "down" way can also apply to the love argument I gave you a couple of letters ago. The "down" way would be to first try to prove that God exists and then deduce some of His attributes, His perfections, one of which would be the perfection of love. That's the more usual logical order. But we could also reverse the order, as I did, and argue "up" from love to God: if love is the meaning of life, mustn't it go "all the way up"? I suspect you'd prefer the more logical order. Am I right?

Your friend,

Peter

19

Dear Michael,

Let me clear up something I said in the first part of my last letter. When I said that my head and my heart both line up together on the side of faith while your head corrects your heart, I didn't mean that this counted as a good logical *argument* for believing the faith any more than it would for believing in Santa Claus. Nor was I claiming any kind of psychological superiority. I admire your honesty in not ignoring your head even though it would make you happy to do so. Do I detect a kind of psychological regret, though, and maybe even envy, because the two deepest parts of my soul agree while the two deepest parts of yours don't? It doesn't make either of us automatically either better or right, of course.

You're quite right in saying that my "argument up" from Jesus's human trustability to belief in God is "least likely to succeed" with an atheist. The reason is obvious: if there is no God, Jesus can't be God. So no arguments about who Jesus is are very likely to change an atheist's mind about whether God exists—although that is possible and has occasionally happened. I think Arthur Katz is an instance of it. So even if I refuted your "fourth hypothesis" about who Jesus is—just a good man who was so mis-understood that he was "divinized" by his disciples, sort of like Monty Python's "Brian"—even if I refuted that conclusively, that would not refute or even put a serious dent in your atheism. So I won't push the argument that it's almost impossible that twelve *Jews* would make that mistake, as pagans or Hindus might, even though I think that's pretty obviously true. If it's logical to be an atheist, then it can't be logical to be a Christian, no matter what the arguments for Christ are. "God does not exist and Jesus is His divine Son" makes sense only as a joke. Yet Jesus is some kind of relevant data, or evidence, though not logical proof.

You are also right in saying that I have assumed the burden of proof and therefore must give you a "compelling reason for faith in God." "Faith" here must mean merely the intellectual belief that God exists rather than the stronger kind of "faith" that includes personal trust and love. That's much less susceptible of logical, deductive proof. But the first is a precondition for the second; you can't love or trust somebody you don't believe exists. Even if argument can get you only to the weaker kind of "faith," intellectual faith, which is not sufficient for the relationship of *religion*, yet that first kind of faith is necessary, even though not suffi-cient. And if argument is necessary to bring you there, then argument is a necessary prerequisite for religion, for the fuller kind of "faith." The Bible itself commands all Christians to "be ready to give a reason for the hope that is in you."

The most obvious arguments for God, it seems to me, are the cosmological arguments, arguments from the evidence in the physical cosmos. Some of these are philosophical arguments about change, causality, contingency, degrees of perfection, and design (Aquinas's famous "five ways"). Others, which Aquinas knew nothing about, stem from modern scientific data, especially big bang cosmology and the anthropic principle.

The more interesting arguments, to me anyway, are what we could call the existential arguments, or the psychological arguments, arguments from the inner, subjective, or immaterial pole of our experience rather than the outer, objective, material objects in the cosmos. I mean our personhood, our minds, our knowledge of truth, our obligation to moral goodness, our love of beauty, and our desire for joy.

There are also historical arguments, which you probably want to omit because they can only be probable, history not being an exact science: for example, arguments from miracles, from the history of the Jews, from Jesus's resurrection, and perhaps from the lives and psychology of the saints and from religious experience. But if you're interested, let's look at them too.

There are also forms of the "ontological argument" which I already told you I reject as fallacious, though it is very clever. It assumes only the definition of God as the being that lacks no conceivable perfection, and argues from that premise alone to His real existence, since real, objective, independent existence is a conceivable perfection, and more perfect than merely subjective, mental existence dependent on a mind. I've never heard of any atheist who was converted by that argument (although Bertrand Russell says in his autobiography that he was once convinced by it for about ten minutes). We all know, intuitively, that you can't get reality out of a concept alone any more than you can get blood out of a stone. You need premises about reality to prove a conclusion about reality.

So where in this menu would you like to begin?

Your friend,

Peter

20

Dear Michael,

No, I'm not sorry you "really don't want to go through the standard arguments for the existence of God, starting with Aquinas's 'five ways.'" In fact, I'm glad you don't, (1) because they're so familiar to me that explaining them wouldn't be much of a challenge, wouldn't break new ground, and (2) because I believe you when you say you have already taken a good look at them, in fact taken a course on them in college and found them "less than compelling," and (3) because I agree that it would turn our letters into a philosophy class. Nothing wrong with a philosophy class in philosophy class, but letters should be letters. A review of those arguments would probably be too familiar, too abstract, and too technical for these more friendly and personal letters.

Instead, I propose we go more deeply into just a few of the arguments that intrigue you the most. If you want to skip the metaphysical-cosmological arguments, how about one or two of the following other ones?

> (1) the argument from truth, Augustine's argument: our temporal minds know eternal truths like 2 + 2 = 4 or

justice; doesn't this indicate the existence of an eternal mind?

(2) The argument from mind: mind can't be caused merely by matter, and human minds exist, therefore they must have some immaterial, mental (or supramental), not sub-mental, cause.

(3) The argument from the validity of reason. Did you read C. S. Lewis's *Miracles* in your course? The argument is tricky, but its basic point is simple: Why trust our minds if they evolved from blind matter alone? Would you trust a computer programmed by chance?

(4) The moral argument, in any of its various forms. For example, real laws indicate real lawgivers with reason and will as their cause, and moral laws are real laws. Or the argument from conscience: even moral relativists have one absolute: it's always wrong to deliberately disobey your own individual moral conscience. *Why*, if conscience is only the voice of society, or parents, or genes, or natural selection? Why treat it as an absolute?

(5) A more difficult but deeper argument is from personhood, or selfhood, or I-hood. Where did that come from, if not from a primary person, an "I AM"?

(6) The argument from beauty is the favorite one of many of my students: there exists the music of Bach (or Mozart, or Beethoven, or Chopin); therefore, there is a God. You either see that or you don't. You either feel the force of that all at once or not at all.

(7) The argument from desire (C. S. Lewis's *Sehnsucht*): we all desire not just pleasure or happiness but joy—a joy

we have never experienced and can't even properly imagine or even conceive and define, except negatively (for example, no pain, death, sin, hate, or boredom). Why do we have this desire for joy unless we are "programmed" for it? All other natural desires bespeak corresponding real objects; why is there only one exception to this rule, namely, the most important desire of all, the desire for total joy, which implies a perfect being and union with this perfect being, in other words, God and Heaven?

(8) The evidence from modern physics. How can there be a big bang without a big banger? Nothing in the universe can cause itself; how can the universe as a whole cause itself? This argument also seems to prove that God is immaterial, since all matter (and time and space) comes after and is dependent on the big bang, not before it. (There *is* no "before" time itself.)

(9) Or the anthropic principle, an updated version of the argument from design in nature. The fact that so many extremely narrow windows of opportunity for human life to emerge in the universe had to be opened at exactly the right time and in the right way, *and were*, certainly looks like a plot, not an accident. The author's fingerprints are all over his manuscript.

(10) There's even an instinctive argument (which, since it's instinctive, isn't really an argument): that Plato must be right, that there must be exits from the cave, that there must be *more*—more things, not less, than are dreamed of in your philosophy, Horatio.

Unless you have a better suggestion, may I suggest we pick two or three of these and toss them back and forth? Are there any that catch your eye? Numbers 4 through 7 seem the most exciting to me.

Your friend,
Peter

21

Dear Michael,

Yes, we should indeed look at arguments *against* God and religion too, for example, "the war between science and religion" (which I maintain does not exist and is a total myth), and difficult doctrines like hell (which I have to admit gets more terrifying the more you look at it), and the Trinity (which I maintain gets more reasonable the more you look at it), and "the terrifying primitivism of the Old Testament and the Koran" (but is it fair to expect *sophistication* from "primitives"? Don't kids have to learn justice before they can learn mercy?), and "all the harm religion has done in history" (like the Ten Commandments or the love ethic of Jesus?) and "whether morality is purer with or without religion" (which sounds to me like "whether a building is purer without a foundation"). And we should take time to focus on your faith (atheism) as much as mine and explore what atheism means and entails for life as well as what religious belief means and entails. The only question is whether we should look at all that evidence for atheism and against religion before or after looking at some of the evidence *for* God and religion. I assumed that the natural logical order would be to look at the belief (in God) first and then the objections to it, especially since we agreed that I had the burden of proof. But if you have strong reasons for the opposite order, let's look at the antitheist case first. I have no set-in-stone agenda.

I'm glad you too find arguments 4 through 7, the more personal or "existential" arguments, "the most interesting, even if not the most scientific or tightly logical."

And I'm glad we can finally get down to the arguments instead of just talking about doing it. So far I'm afraid we've been sounding like two kids spending half the evening arguing about where to go this evening, about where the action is. (Did you do that in college too?) Because of this, our letters have been getting shorter and shorter.

Your friend,
Peter

22

Dear Michael,

Again you surprise me, and again I agree with you. You surprise me by coming to the very edge of the water (the water being a symbol of the arguments for and against God) and then, at the last minute, as we are ready finally to plunge in, remembering one more thing to think about before getting wet. But it is a reasonable thing to think about: that all our philosophical discussions are going to be interpreted very differently by the two of us because you are suspicious of philosophy's claims to know truth and confident only of science, while I am confident of both. You are too honest to pretend that this difference is not there, so you want to confront it. Good, even though it means we postpone for at least one more letter our long-desired swim in the ocean of philosophical arguments. I think you are quite right in insisting that we take a step back and confront this more primordial issue first. Maybe we will come to a better understanding of each other, of where we are each "coming from" and why; and maybe by doing that we will even come to a better understanding of the objective issue we want to argue (theism vs. atheism). It's at least worth a try.

The question that divides us is whether there is any reliable knowledge outside of science, especially in philosophy and/or in common sense. I am tempted to do a *philosophical* analysis of the question, but I'm resisting that temptation (1) because we already discussed that under the label of "scientism" and (2) because it would involve us in technical questions of epistemology, especially your presuppositions of nominalism and empiricism, and that would take a long time, for the clearest way to do that is by a tour through the history of modern philosophy to see the natural development and consequences of nominalism through the six centuries from Ockham to logical positivism. Instead of all that history, let's just look at a single *logical* point.

We are centering our discussion on atheism versus theism, no God versus God. Two very different "worldviews." *You* see the difference between these two worldviews as the difference between science on the one hand and religious faith on the other hand. I don't. I see the difference as the difference between a man looking through a telescope and a man looking through binoculars. I use two lenses; you use only one. We both believe in science, but you do not believe in religion or even in philosophy, or in metaphysics, at least.

That's why I'm glad you stopped us from jumping into the water of argument before we had confronted this point, which should come first: *Is our difference a difference between science and religion?* Are we coming at this issue of God from opposite presuppositions—you from "science only" and I from "faith also"? From what I just said about binoculars, you might think I agree that that is our deepest difference, but I say that is *not* so. In fact, I say that that is not even the right definition of our difference at all. And I have two reasons for saying that. First, I am not the only one who has faith: you have unproved assumptions, or faith, just as much as I do. And second, you are not the only one who uses science as a method of thinking. I do too, not only in science but also in religion. In other words, I have a broader definition of "science" than you do. It's not your science versus my faith; it's your faith versus my faith and your science versus my science.

If "faith" means "assumptions or presuppositions that are necessary to ground subsequent arguments and which themselves are not proved, or cannot be proved or demonstrated with certainty," then I say that you have, and need, and use faith just as much as I do. Here are some of the tenets of your faith: you believe

(1) That the world the science explores really exists and is not a dream or an illusion, as some Hindus and Buddhists say.

(2) That your mind can know this world, that the laws of thought correspond to the laws of things.

(3) That nature is uniform and reliable and will not change its fundamental laws tomorrow. (Even Hume confessed this puzzled him: the uniformity of nature is presupposed in all inductive scientific reasoning, yet it cannot be proved inductively.)

(4) That effects must have sufficient causes; that nothing just pops into existence for no reason at all. If a large blue rabbit suddenly appeared on your head, you would not say, "Oh well, large blue rabbits just happen."

(5) That the laws of logic are universally and necessarily true for everything.

(6) That you yourself, your mind, your personhood, your "I" are real.

Descartes did not really prove the objective fact that he existed by his famous "I think, therefore I am." Though

I find it personally impossible to doubt my own existence, I find it quite easy to doubt his existence, as he finds it easy to doubt mine. A second reason why "I think" does not *prove* "I exist" is because the "I" of the conclusion ("I exist") is presupposed in the premise ("I think"), so he is logically begging the question.

I don't say that we don't *know* any of these things with certainty, but I say we cannot *prove* them. And if "faith" means simply "accepting something without proof," they are all matters of faith, though not explicitly *religious* faith.

They are not all in the same boat. I think we can be *absolutely* certain, indubitably certain, of the premises of arguments 5 and 6 even though we cannot prove them. The laws of logic (number 5) are objectively self-evident and logically indubitable, and my own existence (number 6) is subjectively self-evident and psychologically indubitable. No one denies 5 and 6. Yet 5 and 6 are not *provable.* The "faith" you use to accept them is not an explicitly religious faith, a faith in a God; yet it is "faith," by your definition of faith that I quoted in the previous paragraph.

My second point is that I am as scientific as you are. Here we get into my broader definition of "science."

I divide the sciences into four classes: mathematical sciences, physical sciences, human sciences, and philosophical sciences.

They are different in that the mathematical sciences use only deductive reasoning, not induction or sense observation; the physical sciences use a combination of induction and deduction and begin with sensory observation; the human sciences are inexact rather than exact, so they claim probability rather than certainty;

and the philosophical sciences do not limit their subject matter as much as the other sciences do: metaphysics deals with all beings, epistemology with all knowledge, philosophical anthropology with all men, ethics with all good and evil, and so on.

But all four kinds of science use causal reasoning. All four test hypotheses by how well they explain data. All four subject themselves to the scrutiny of reason; they demand good logical reasons for their judgments. Philosophy does this just as much as the empirical sciences do.

Of course, there is a lot of irrational philosophy, fake philosophy, bad philosophy. But that does not invalidate good philosophy any more than fake or bad physical science invalidates good science. Even if *most* philosophy is bad while most physical science is good, that would not invalidate philosophy as such. Even if it's easier to get away with falsehoods in philosophy than in the other sciences (except politics!), that defect is balanced by a different but equally important advantage: that philosophy's questions are much more important than those of any other science.

You will probably reply that scientists at least reach agreement, while philosophers do not. But scientists disagree too; and the more important the science, the more disagreement there is. There's more disagreement about infinite numbers than about finite numbers, and more disagreement about cosmology than about chemistry, and more disagreement about psychology than about biology. You see the pattern? There are two variables. The more important and the more difficult a science is, the more disagreement there is. So the fact that philosophers disagree the most indicates the importance and the difficulty of philosophy's questions. It does not invalidate them.

23

Dear Michael,

I'm glad you said, "I'll get on your philosophy boat with you even though I'm not totally convinced it's not doomed to sink." Your choice, I think, illustrates the important truth in William James's "pragmatism." Sometimes practice has to run ahead of theory in order to test the theory. For instance, to test and validate your neighbor's goodwill, you have to assume his goodwill rather than using the scientific method on him and treating him with suspicion until he gives you goodwill, because suspicion will *inhibit* his goodwill. Sometimes you have to assume without proof that you can do a thing (like climbing a mountain) before you can actually do it, because if you don't have that faith, that confidence in yourself, you won't be able to do it.

So let's look at the "argument from desire" that you picked out. You say you picked it because you think it's at the same time the most interesting and the logically weakest of all the arguments for God. You probably think there is a natural connection between these two features, but I think that's an illusion, like the illusion that any music that is very logical and mathematical and carefully structured, like that of Bach, must also be passionless

75

music, and that the wilder and more irrational a work of art is, the more it elicits passion. Not true; it may elicit only pity and contempt. Bach, on the other hand, is mathematicized *passion*.

The argument has a tight logical structure, but its minor premise is not "tight" or logically clear; yet that premise is what makes it so interesting. (So your opposition between clarity and interestingness is true in this case, *within* the argument.) Here's the logical structure of the argument:

> Major premise: All natural, innate, universal human desires correspond to realities that can satisfy them.
> Minor premise: The desire for something that cannot be positively defined and cannot be attained in this world, something that religious believers call God and Heaven (union with God), is a natural, innate, universal human desire.
> Conclusion: Therefore God (and union with God in Heaven) exists.

The major premise seems clear. It does two things. It first distinguishes two kinds of desires. Desires to go to the Land of Oz, or fly like Superman, or for the Cubs to win the World Series, are not natural and innate (they do not come from human nature itself but from some external human artifice) and not universal (Mets fans do not want the Cubs to win). But the desires for food, drink, sex, sleep, beauty, justice, truth, and friendship are all natural, innate, and universal desires. The second thing the major premise does is to note that every single other natural and universal desire corresponds to a real object that can satisfy it. Rocks don't fall in love, people do; fish don't want to fly, birds do; cats don't want to burrow in the ground, worms do.

We may add a reason for this correspondence if we dare, but we don't have to: the reason is "commonsensical" or philosophical: that nature is not random but designed as an ecological system.

The major premise seems clear and undeniable, though not terribly interesting. But it's the minor premise that's fascinating, though it's deniable. Any individual can simply say that he has never felt the desire for anything more than this world can give; that he is perfectly happy; that even the mystics' Heaven could not possibly give him any greater joy than he now has. If he says that, there is no logical way to refute him. He is just small-minded and unimaginative. But you can't refute him, any more than you can refute someone with a migraine headache who insists that he is not in any pain at all. It's not true, but no one else can prove it's not true.

But most of us, if we are honest, know the experience the argument appeals to, even we do not relate it in any way to religion. The premises do not presuppose any religion or religious faith, only external observation (the major premise) and internal experience (the minor premise). The argument does not claim to "prove God" by beginning with some concept of God—any concept of God—and then proving that this "God" exists. It begins only with human experience, a universal human experience: of longing for some *x* that is indefinable and unattainable, or at least not yet defined or attained.

It is like the cosmological arguments this way. Just as the cosmological arguments for God begin merely from the premises about features we all experience in the cosmos (like causality)—

they do *not* begin with a concept of God and then claim to prove that this God is real—so this argument begins simply with a universal human experience. In the case of the cosmological arguments, the experience is external and empirical; in the case of the argument from desire, the experience is internal and not empirical.

In fact, in each of Aquinas's five cosmological arguments, he does not use the word "God" at all until the argument is all over. All the arguments' claims prove is *not* that the God of religion exists but that there must be some unmoved mover, some first cause, some necessary being, some most perfect being, and some intelligent designer. Then Aquinas adds a sentence like "And this is what we call 'God.'" The last sentence is an empirical observation, which notices that some of the attributes of the God that religious believers believe in correspond to the attributes of this x that the argument proves. It is what I call "a very thin slice of God."

The argument from desire is not talking about an unusual "mystical" experience at all but about an experience that all, or nearly all, of us have had, I think. We typically have it not during prayer or any religious exercise but during whatever natural, earthly pleasures stab our heart with desire, not with satisfaction. Ironically, it happens not when we are miserable but when we are happiest. Have you ever read C. S. Lewis's description of it in *The Problem of Pain* or "The Weight of Glory" or his autobiography, *Surprised by Joy*? If not, try it and see if you can "relate to" it.

I trust you won't let your suspicions trump your honesty here. What I mean is that you surely must suspect that perhaps if you do not deny this desire as the "minor premise" of the argument, you may be unable to avoid the conclusion you want to deny, namely God. For the easiest way to refute any argument is to deny its premise.

Think of the most joyful "peak experience" of your life. Maybe it was just the cry of a seagull on a clear winter day, or a suddenly stunning landscape, or a heartbreaking song, or an experience of ecstatic, personal and transpersonal sex. Didn't you sense that all these things were just the smell of the rose, hints of something greater from which they came, fingers pointing to something far greater than themselves, messengers, prophets of a higher God? Didn't it seem as if this "something else" was almost trying to *break through* them?

C. S. Lewis defines the experience this way: "The experience is one of intense longing. It is distinguished from other longings by two things. In the first place, though the sense of want is acute and even painful, yet the mere wanting is felt to be somehow a delight. . . . In the second place, there is a peculiar mystery about the *object* of this desire . . . every one of those supposed objects for the desire is inadequate to it."

His interpretation follows:

> It appeared to me therefore that if a man diligently followed this desire, pursing the false objects until their falsity appeared . . . he must come out at last into the clear knowledge that the human soul was made to enjoy some object that is never fully given—nay, cannot even be imagined as given—in our present mode of subjective and spatio-temporal experience. This Desire was in the soul as the Siege Perilous in Arthur's castle— the chair in which only one could sit. . . . All your life an unattainable ecstasy has hovered just beyond the grasp of your consciousness. The day is coming when you will wake to find,

beyond all hope, that you have attained it, or else, that it was within your reach and you have lost it forever.

Even if you can't identify this positive experience in yourself, surely you understand its negative side, the "lover's quarrel with the world" that we all have, the sense that "this world is not enough" (the title of a James Bond movie). Even if we don't have a desire for Heaven, we all have a dissatisfaction with earth. Would we really want to live here *forever*? Wouldn't artificial immortality by genetic engineering be more of a threat than a promise? After a million years, who wouldn't be bored?

What do we want? Something "eye has not seen, ear has not heard nor has it entered into the heart of man." Something "mystical." How about infinite, incomprehensible, immortal, intensely passionate ecstasy? If you don't believe in this, don't you at least hope for it? If you don't hope for it, don't you at least wish for it, dream about it?

Your friend,
Peter

24

Dear Michael,

Yes, I expected you would "find the premise more interesting than the argument." I think all of us (except convinced pessimists) are more readily persuaded of the truth of a conclusion when we *want* to be persuaded; and we want to be persuaded when we "identify with" the premise, that is, when we understand it from having experienced it ourselves. This is true of the cosmological premises as well as the experiential premises: the argument from motion would be less convincing to a blind paralytic. So the very premise that is the argument's weak point (because it is deniable) is also its strong point, its attraction. That is why, even though you think the "demonstrative power of this 'proof' is nearly zero," you are attracted to it; you chose it as the one you wanted to look at first.

But as to the "demonstrative power," there are only three things, as you know, that can impede the demonstration of the certain truth of the conclusion of a syllogism: an ambiguously used term, a false premise, or a logical fallacy. Obviously there is no formal logical fallacy in the syllogism. And you have not pointed out any ambiguous term. So you will have to deny a premise. Which one?

There are only two. If you cannot honestly deny the minor premise (which simply affirms that we have this experience of a desire in our nature for something more than this world can satisfy), then you will have to deny the major premise, the only other assumption. That is the universal principle that every natural desire points to a real object.

You will probably do this by saying (if I may play the prophet) that just because all *other* natural desires correspond to real objects (which we know to be true by experience and inductive generalization), that does not mean that *this* one will. Inductive arguments from "some" to "all" are never certain. You could argue that just because all other books on my bookcase except my Plato book are paperbacks, that does not prove either that my Plato book is a paperback or that all the books on my bookcase are paperbacks.

That is true in this case, but only because there is no natural or necessary connection between being on my bookcase and being a paperback rather than a hardcover. The predicate is accidental to the subject. But in the classic syllogism "All men are mortal, and Socrates is a man; therefore, Socrates is mortal," we cannot use that same skeptical demurral, as John Stuart Mill tried to do to show that the syllogism was a fake. He argued that we could not know that *all* men are mortal until *after* we knew that Socrates was mortal, for if Socrates proved to be not mortal, our universal major premise would be disproved. So, he claimed, the syllogism doesn't really go forward but backward: we could not know the major premise before, but only after, knowing the conclusion. But that argument mistakenly assumes (1) that only induction, not deduction, is reliable, and (2) that the relation between mortality and humanity is as accidental as the relation between being on my bookcase and being a paperback.

Mill was a nominalist and did not believe there were any such things as universal natures or essences like humanity or bookness, so he has no doctrine of the "predicables" as Aristotle has. The "predicables" distinguish five possible relationships between the predicate of any proposition and the subject, based on the predicate's relation to the essence of the subject. (Yes, I know this assumes that there are such things as essences and does not prove that assumption. But Mill equally assumes the opposite and does not prove his assumption either. And common sense makes that assumption. That's why there are common nouns as well as proper nouns.)

(1) A *species* is the whole essence of the subject, for example, "Man is a rational animal."

(2) A *genus* is the general, or generic, or common aspect of the essence, for example, "Man is an animal."

(3) The *specific difference* is the specific, differentiating aspect of the essence, for example, "Man is rational."

(4) A *property*, or *proper accident*, is a predicate that is not the essence but is caused by the essence, for example, "Man creates art," or "Man knows good and evil," or "Man invents science."

(5) An *accident* is a predicate that is not part of the essence and not caused by the essence, for example, "Some men are English," or "Man is often bald," or "No man is over fourteen feet tall."

Because Mill does not distinguish accidental and essential predicables, he does not distinguish the two cases, the "all men are mortal" syllogism and the "all the books on my bookcase are paperbacks" syllogism.

Here's how this logical distinction answers the skeptical objection to the major premise of the argument from desire. The reason we know the major premise to be true is not that we have observed empirically every single example of desires and done a complete induction but that we have understood the relation between the predicate and the subject. To have a real object is a *property* (in the Aristotelian sense, in the "predicables") of all innate, natural desires. Desires for nonexistent things like the Land of Oz come from external things like movies or advertisements, but desires for real things come from our human nature. It would make no sense for our very nature to desire something that doesn't exist.

In a nihilistic, existentialist, meaningless, irrational universe, that could happen. But in a rational universe, a universe in which each creature is in an intelligible relationship to its environment, we find that in every creature each natural hunger corresponds to a natural food. And we find in ourselves alone a natural hunger for something more than nature can provide, something like God and union with God. Is that an absolutely undeniable proof that God exists? No. But the price you pay for saying no is that you have given up a rational universe for an irrational universe.

The fact that all the other desires correspond to real foods can't be accidental. Either we're being lured on by a good God who uses these appetizers to whet our appetite for the main course, Himself, or else we're being lured on by a cruel, clever spirit who, after all the appetizers have made us hungry for the main course, provides us in the end, after death, with—nothing.

You see, it's like the argument from the human brain as a computer: either it's programmed by chance, by a good mind, or by a bad mind. So here: our desires and their one-to-one relationship to reality were caused either by unintelligent chance, or by a good creator, or by a bad one. If chance is an irrational explanation, your only choice is between God and the devil.

I know you will find this a very "soft" argument. It's not like the arguments in math or physics. It's not quantifiable, and it's not empirically provable (until after death), but it has an empirical data base in both premises.

The only other way to escape this argument is to deny the minor premise. But in the very act of choosing this argument and confessing that it intrigues you, you have implicitly confessed that you have experienced this desire, that you admit that it exists.

I await your reply. I don't expect a knock on my door at midnight and a demand to be baptized. I don't know what I expect. Probably the unexpected, again.

Your friend,
Peter

25

Dear Michael,

Yes, I suppose you could say the argument is only a "clue" or a "probability," since "we can only reason by analogy from other desires." But at least that's something. It's a pointing finger, which it's not simply irrational to trust, as I do (*and* not simply irrational *not* to trust, as you do).

And *all* arguments are arguments from analogy in a sense. Analogy is just a shortcut way of moving from "Mr. *X*, Mrs. *Y*, and Mrs. *Z* are mortal" to "Socrates is mortal" by bypassing the two logical steps of induction (from *X, Y,* and *Z* "up" to all men) and then deduction ("down" from all men to Socrates). The crucial question is whether there is such a thing as intellectual intuition or understanding of the analogy or likeness between *X, Y,* and *Z* and Socrates: Can we meaningfully ask the question whether they share the same essential nature or whether the resemblance is only accidental? Nominalists say no, we can't make that distinction between the essential and the accidental, because there are no real universal essences and therefore no such thing as an intellectual intuition into them. That's why nominalists like Hume and Mill are skeptical of both deductive syllogisms and analogies.

How does this apply to our disagreement about the argument from desire? Does it mean that if you agree with my logical or epistemological point here, then the difference between us is not a logical difference or an empirical difference but a psychological difference? Is it simply that I am more ready than you to trust analogies, or "clues," or "pointing fingers," if that is all the argument really is, as you say? I think we should not assume that either your tendency to trust less or my tendency to trust more is in itself good or bad. For if we assume more trust, we are more likely to end up with God, and if we assume less trust, we are less likely to end up with God. The converse is also true: if God exists, you trust too little; if God doesn't exist, I trust too much. Trust justifies God, and God justifies trust. So we can't use trust as our premise to a conclusion about God, because we will be begging the question either way. Yet each position is consistent: if God exists, then we should trust; and if we trust, we will probably conclude that God exists. And if God does not exist, then we should not trust that much, and if we do not trust that much, then we will probably not conclude that God exists.

You argue that "atheism is more humanistic, more complimentary to humanity. For suppose God does not exist. Then we invented him. What a creative invention that is! What a great fantasy! It does great credit to us! But if we did not invent him, but he invented us, that does no credit to us at all. A parallel case: suppose we discovered that Shakespeare did not invent *Hamlet* but discovered it already written. That would lessen Shakespeare's greatness. So atheism increases Man's greatness and theism lessens it."

I disagree. A mankind who inhabits a universe great enough to manifest a God is a greater species, not a lesser one, than a mankind who invented a fictional God to compensate for the failure of reality to provide one. We are raised, not lowered, in the presence of the truly great; we are lowered only in the presence of a tyrant. You're not greater when you invent fantasy food on a desert island than when you eat real food in a great restaurant. We are taller in a cathedral than in a cellar.

To respond to your example, let's argue not about Hamlet, since we don't know whether he is real or fictional, but about something we know to be a fictional invention, and not a reality—dragons, say, or unicorns, or Tolkien's elves. Surely it would be a more wonderful world and life if we discovered that they were real. To live in a greater world rather than a lesser one—that ennobles us. So to live in a world created and designed by God, a world that comes from God and leads back to Him and Heaven and eternal ecstasy and light—surely that is better, greater, nobler, than to live in a world where we are merely the accidental burp of primordial slime and doomed to return forever to the dirt of the earth from which we just happened to blindly evolve, with no hope of God or Heaven! We are not ennobled by the demeaning of everything else. We are not rivals of everything else. We're not on a cosmic seesaw, with the universe going up when we go down and down when we go up. Your argument seems to assume this terrible premise.

I went to the beach yesterday. It was glorious: very blue sky, very yellow sun, very white cirrus clouds, very birdy seabirds, very hot and sandy sand, very wet and salty water, and very big waves. (On one of them I totally wiped out and somersaulted twice over myself like an acrobat!) The bigger and better the world is, the bigger and better we are. You feel as if you *belong* in such a world, you are proud to be part of such a world, at the same time that you feel humble and grateful to its creator. Do you understand that feeling, at least, even if you don't believe its theology?

Do you want to argue about another argument now, or more about this one, or something else?

Your friend,

Peter

26

Dear Michael,

I now see why you so quickly admitted that the God idea was "too good to be true," even though that involved you in a deep existential problem about the dividedness of the human heart if its two deepest ideals, goodness (God) and truth (reality), lead in opposite directions. You do understand the experience Lewis calls *Sehnsucht* (longing), and you understand why it leads some people to believe in God.

I would call that "the way of hope," not "the way of faith," for faith, though it does not need Clifford's kind of evidence in order to be rational, does demand *some* sort of evidence to make the object of faith *probable*; but hope only needs *possibility*. You can't hope for the impossible, but you can hope for the surprising and the apparently improbable. And of course the desire in itself is not a proof or even an argument; yet the "argument from desire" does claim to be a proof, and you have not yet refuted it.

You mention Plato's cave, the most famous image in the history of philosophy. I think you understand why it is so famous because you understand the deep things in the human heart that it appeals to. Unlike most philosophers, who interpret it only as an intellectual theory in metaphysics and epistemology—the objective reality of universals or class concepts, Plato's "theory of forms" or "theory of (Platonic) Ideas"—you connect it with *Sehnsucht*, the mysterious longing for something we've never had and can't define. I think you are profoundly right there, even though you think that the world outside the cave is only Plato's "dream" rather than a reality.

I think you are quite right, and quite profound, in connecting it with heart, love, desire, hope, and so on, rather than merely a theory about ideas (or Ideas). It hits the heart, not just the head. We desperately *want* there to be a world outside the cave. We want Hamlet to be right when he says, "There are *more* things in heaven and earth, Horatio, than are dreamed of in your philosophy." Postmodernist nihilism and its "hermeneutic of suspicion" says there is *less*.

Perhaps that's part of the hidden attraction of the fine arts, especially the most "mystical" of them, music. They are "signals of transcendence," fingers pointing beyond themselves toward exits from the cave. That's what explains why my students' favorite argument for God is the argument from the music of Bach, and why I know three ex-atheists (two of them philosophers and one a poet and a monk) who said they were converted away from atheism by Bach's *St. Matthew Passion*. It's not just sentimentalism; it's an intellectual intuition: the music we have in our soul just has to match the music outside our soul. There has to be more.

Not that it's not a great cave. But there has to be more. We see this with most conviction not when we are poor and in pain, when the cave is smallest and darkest and most uncomfortable. It's precisely at those moments when we feel the cave's greatness the most, when we are most open to the charms and beauties of our physical and emotional universe, that we feel this "divine discontent," this "lover's quarrel with the world."

I am frankly surprised that you understand and feel this so well yet are still an atheist. Most atheists I've talked to about this, and about the argument from desire, respond by denying the minor premise of the argument, namely, the existence of such a desire. They say they are totally and perfectly content to be successful yuppies in this world. They say they feel no desire to leave the cave.

I think that's because they simply cannot imagine what the world outside the cave could be. And that's a possible argument against it. No one can say what a perfect Heaven would be, one that would never get boring. I find it fascinating that there has never been a really moving picture of Heaven—in movies, in novels, or even in theology, except for the most abstract and negative concepts (no death, no pain, no evil, no misunderstanding, no hate, no injustice—and yet no boredom). It's unimaginable. We don't know what it is we are desiring. And yet some of us confess that we desire it. And others suppress the desire because they don't know what it is; they find it intellectually meaningless since it is so unimaginable.

I've gone on about the *Sehnsucht* argument because I think you are as fascinated with it as I am. But I've already presented the logical force of it, and you've already said it doesn't convince you because it seems much more likely that its data (the *Sehnsucht* itself) can be explained by wishful thinking than by a real God and Heaven.

This is like Hume's argument against miracles: he argued that it's more likely that all the reports of miracles are explainable as lies or hallucinations, since both of these, unlike miracles, are quite common, like the laws of nature themselves which they obey. But of course this begs the question, for if miracles happen, they are by definition uncommon. So is each individual human being's genetic code. Does that mean they cannot exist? Similarly, if Heaven exists, it is also uncommon, in fact unique. So you can't argue that it is "more likely" that there is no world outside the cave, no supernatural world in addition to nature, than that there is. "More likely" by what standard? The standards of the cave? Of course it is. By definition. To argue that the regularities inside the cave prove that there is nothing outside the cave is like the fish in a little fishbowl judging how unlikely or impossible it is that there is an ocean full of whales and sharks and other weird things outside the little fishbowl, by using the standards of the fishbowl.

So where do we go from here?

Your friend,

Peter

27

Dear Michael,

You don't want to let this one go, do you? Okay, fine. Neither do I.

Are you aware of what you sound like when you try to refute my argument from desire? You sound like you are arguing *for* theism and *for* the argument from desire. How? When you correct me and say that I am wrong to say that there could not possibly be evidence inside the cave, or the fishbowl, that proves or disproves the existence of a greater world outside it. And I think you are right there, and I retract my mistake. There is at least relevant data. In fact, all the theistic arguments do just that: find data in the world for the existence of a being "outside" the world.

The data you offer as an example of such evidence, you think, does not prove God—in fact you think that none of the evidence does. But at least you admit that there is some evidence for Him, and I admit there is some evidence against Him (evil, evil believers, injustice, etc.). You mention the evidence or data that I myself offered to you in a previous letter and then forgot about, namely, the data of the human heart, that it demands two things absolutely: truth and goodness. I then asked: How could the human heart be so badly split that our two deepest desires lead in opposite directions?—which they do if atheism is true, for the absolute truth is that there is no God of absolute goodness. How could the heart of the heart not correspond to the heart of objective reality? How could our desire for truth about reality and our desire for goodness and beauty and justice and love lead in opposite directions? How could it be that the more loving we become, the stupider we become? How could it be that the smarter you get, the less saintly you get? How could the saints—I mean the real saints, those who love goodness the most—be the most wrong about truth? For they are the most convinced that God is real, that the absolute truth *is* absolute goodness. Is Jesus the stupidest person who ever lived? No one ever loved and trusted and obeyed and guided his life by and depended on the reality of God more than He did. Was He history's biggest fool? How could it be that the better a person you become, the more likely it is that you will be wrong and deluded about the most important thing of all? How could love and intelligence contradict each other?

I am embarrassed to admit that you took that argument more seriously than I did. You put this "Platonism of the heart," as you call it, in very clear and moving terms, though only in order to refute it as an error, which you tried to do by Freud's "wish fulfillment" hypothesis, which you find "very reasonable." But I detect more passion in the "error" than in its "refutation." You already sound more like a C. S. Lewis than like a Bertrand Russell.

I think you are falling in love with God under another name. The named God you thought you believed in as a child, the God you "inherited" from your parents, was not the real God, and therefore He was not real to you either. The real God is presently anonymous to you but anonymously present to you. I make this

28

Dear Michael,

Again you surprise me. Instead of choosing one or more arguments (or none), you tell me about what you call a "kind of experiment." You say it was only your fascination with art, and its "pull" on the heart, and your "scientific" desire to explore that "deep and dark psychological well" that led you into the cathedral last Monday. Perhaps; but you know as well as I do that there are things going on at the bottom of that well that are not only subconscious but maybe even sub-subconscious.

So you went into a Catholic church and sat down in front of the tabernacle on the high altar, knowing what Catholics believe about what was really in it—Jesus Christ Himself, in person, God incarnate, hiding under the appearance of a little piece of bread. You say that your "mind found, and still finds, that doctrine radically unlikely, improbable, fantastic, unbelievable." Fine. Naturally. What drew you there, then? "Just to be very quiet for a few moments—that's easy to do inside a church—to observe what motives are moving around in the well of my psyche."

As a scientist, you say you were "gathering data in order to test a hypothesis about the human heart, not about God, since one

97

does not test hypotheses about entities one believes do not exist."
Fine. But if God does exist, you cannot thus safely separate the
"hypothesis" of God from any hypothesis about the heart that He
made in His image and as His inner prophet. There was risk in
that experiment.

You then go on to say that the hypothesis you were exploring
was "not just psychological but in a sense cosmological as well: it
was, I think, the hypothesis that this beautiful cathedral is like a
piece of music, and that people spent enormous effort, time, and
money constructing it because something in the heart wants to
listen to this music—that's all." Frankly, that last "that's all" sounds
suspiciously like "The lady doth protest too much, methinks."

So you knew you were "not just inside brick and stone, but
something like being inside a symphony orchestra while it was
playing a symphony." And you interpret this beauty as "a cover
for the emptiness inside, like the gold overlay on the tabernacle:
so flashingly beautiful that it effectively conceals the fact that what
is inside is only bread and not God." So you think you have solved
the puzzle of why the churches and the art and the music of
believers is so beautiful, if what they believe is so wrong: it's a
diversion, a fake, a facade.

But doesn't the beauty there look *true* rather than ornamental;
substantial rather than a facade? And the music that you so identify
with the architecture ("frozen music," someone called it)—what
kind of music was it? Was it fake? Was it mechanical? Was it
manipulative? Was it music made just by a blind material universe
which accidentally evolved human hearts and minds as its instruments? No. It was music played by material instruments, but those
material instruments were played by spiritual persons, not vice
versa. In your worldview, persons are the instruments of a blind,

nonspiritual universe. In my worldview, it's the reverse. Which worldview makes more sense of music? Didn't the "frozen music" in that cathedral sound or look like a chorus of human voices? Didn't it sound like human voices singing a capella, directly, and without any instruments at all except their own bodies?

You sound like someone very sensitive to music and to the difference between shallow, fake, manipulative music and deep, profound, authentic music. Which kind of music did you actually hear before you started thinking and constructing hypotheses and arguments? How much attention did you pay to your data?

Your friend,

Peter

29

Dear Michael,

Of course it's not a logical argument: "The cathedral looked pretty; therefore, God exists." But it's something; it's data that has to be explained. And the data is not that "the cathedral looked pretty." Dresses on teenage girls are "pretty." What you saw was *beauty*. And it wasn't just a "feeling." You *saw* it, with your eyes, your heart, and your mind all working together. At least get your data straight before you argue about hypotheses.

Of course there are hypotheses that explain the data without any kind of God. You can always find them or make them if you want to. If you died today and found yourself in a celestial city with golden streets and saw a "being of light" with a human face, you could even then formulate an atheistic hypothesis to explain it as a hallucination. You can also invent a "hallucination" hypothesis *now* to explain the world you see every day, the world of matter and change and plurality. Some Hindus and Buddhists do just that and believe it. But is it the best hypothesis? Many hypotheses "save the appearances" or explain the data, but which hypothesis does the *most* justice to *all* the data? Isn't that how a scientist is supposed to think?

That's not an easy and quick question to answer, even in a limited and well-defined area of science. Why should it be any easier or quicker when it comes to the God hypothesis that claims to be the "theory of everything"?

Okay, enough. Next you want to look at other arguments, all three kinds of arguments—epistemological, moral, and cosmological—rather than picking just one. Good. That means looking at all the data, as a good scientist would insist on doing, rather than playing with just your favorite one, as a debater would do to win the debate.

So let's start with the most technical, philosophical, elusive, dull, abstract, and purely cerebral kind of arguments, the epistemological ones about *truth* and *mind* and *reason*. Those three words are at the center of three arguments.

First, the one from truth. This comes from St. Augustine. We know many truths that are changeable and changing, like "Caesar crossed the Rubicon," and "Earth supports life," which wasn't true a billion years ago and won't be true a billion years from now, and even "F = MA," which wasn't true during the first few seconds after the big bang. But we also know some truths that are unchangeable, like "Effects require causes," and "2 + 2 = 4." Yet everything in our subjective knowing apparatus—mind, reason, experience, sensation—and everything in the objective material universe we know—matter, time, space, energy—is changing. How can our changing minds know unchangeable truth? That's a puzzle in our data. Perhaps the existence of an eternal divine mind is not the *only* hypothesis that explains that piece of data, but it's certainly a natural one and a deservedly popular one. And I can't imagine a better one. Can you? If so, can you tell me how it is better without *presupposing* atheism, scientism, naturalism, or materialism?

A second argument is from the existence of our minds. Our minds can't be explained by matter alone. Matter has intelligibility but not intelligence; it is a thinkable object but not a thinking subject. The mind is more than the physical brain. For we can think about the brain—indeed, cybernetics is a highly detailed science—and thinking about x has to transcend x, has to be more than x. (I should say "knowing" rather than just "thinking" because I mean "true thinking.") Therefore, the mind is more than the brain.

Mind can't be explained merely by matter, no matter how complex the matter. Material complexity can't explain conscious thought. Only persons, I's, minds, souls can think. They *use* their brains, as we use computers; but the brain by itself, like a computer by itself, can't think any more than a rock can think. A brain is much more *complex* than a rock, but so is a very large building made out of rocks more complex than a single rock. But it's not even a little closer to thinking than a single rock. Consider the following series of entities, each of which is more complex than the one before it: an abacus, an adding machine, a cell phone, a small computer, a supercomputer, a brain in a vat. Where does consciousness begin?

I'm opening a big new can of worms here called "philosophy of mind," but I just want to make this one simple and obvious point: that there's somebody home as long as we're alive. When we die, we leave the house, including the brain. Everything material in our brain remains, structurally, at least for a short time, but it can't function, it can't think even a little tiny bit, because the person, the mind, the soul suddenly exited from it. My point is that matter can't explain mind; quantitative material complexity can't explain consciousness. It's a qualitative leap. To know matter is to transcend matter.

Let me repeat the simple point I made before: "The knowledge of a thing is not one of that thing's parts." But we can know truths about the whole material universe. Therefore, we are not merely parts of the material iniverse. This refutes both materialism and naturalism, though it doesn't yet prove God.

A third argument is from the validity of reason.

Let's begin by distinguishing two meanings of "because." One thing happens *because* another thing happens: that's material causality, or physical causality, or an "efficient cause." But we can also say that one idea is true *because* another idea is true: that's formal causality, or a logical "because." One billiard ball "causes" another one to move in the first sense of "because," and one set of premises "causes" a conclusion to be true, to logically follow, in the second sense of "because." These two causal relationships are different, and only when the logical "because" corresponds to the physical "because" do we have truth. If we know that an idea can be explained by physical causality without logical causality, we discount it as irrational or nonrational. The drunk sees dragons because he's drunk; the patient hallucinates because a bit of bone is pressing on his brain. "He is scared of dogs because he was bitten very painfully by one when he was two" means "He has no logical reason to be afraid of dogs."

Now what hypothesis best explains what we have discovered so far? That we are simply the most recently evolved parts of the whole physical universe, which is all that there is? Or that there is an eternal, preexisting divine mind which designed both the physical universe and our brains and nervous systems and created human minds to use these physical instruments for their thinking? The second hypothesis is supernaturalism, and it says that whenever we exercise reason, that is, mind in search of truth, we are pulling on something supernatural, using something supernatural, in touch with something supernatural, something that is not simply a part of the physical universe but which can *know* the whole universe.

If you agree with this argument against materialistic naturalism but claim that it does not yet refute atheism, you are probably right. But that means that you are at least a supernaturalist, though not a theist. You call yourself "an atheistic *humanist.*" In that case, you seem already to have taken two-thirds of the journey away from atheism and toward theism. You have seven billion little gods playing with the material universe. Why not add one big God to explain the seven billion little ones? In fact, how else can you explain them? Certainly not by evolution alone, if you have abandoned both materialism and naturalism. That would be like explaining the profundity of *Hamlet* by counting the syllables. The count may be true, but it does not explain the genius of *Hamlet*. Evolution too is probably true—I have no problem with the idea— but its account does not explain the minds that discovered it.

Your friend,

Peter

30

Dear Michael,

Your major objection to my three epistemological arguments is that even if they are valid, their conclusion is so weak and abstract that it is "not two-thirds of the way to theism, as you claim, but not even one-third of the way." Perhaps you are right. The arguments do not yet prove God. That's a quantum leap. Yet, if they are valid, they do prove *something*, however thin it may be. They certainly point in the *direction* of theism more than in the direction of atheism, don't they?

Like you, I am "impatient to get into the more interesting but more messy arguments." So let's look at the rather simple argument that I call the "argument from personhood" and then the much more complex "moral argument."

The "argument from personhood" begins by distinguishing persons from things, knowing subjects from known objects. Persons are entities that have self-consciousness, that can meaningfully refer to themselves as "I," and that can judge themselves and their choices as good or bad. This is a quantum leap from everything subpersonal. An *I* is not a very strange kind of *It* but transcends It-hood in kind, not just in degree. Personhood transcends thing-hood; I-ness transcends It-ness.

That's the minor premise. The major premise is the principle of causality: effects can't transcend their causes. These persons that we are must have been caused by something personal or superpersonal, not subpersonal. Our adequate cause must be something more than the universe that did not contain any persons before we evolved.

Therefore, not despite evolution but precisely because evolution happened, there must be a superhuman mind behind it, using evolution to make images of Himself, somewhat as a computer programmer puts the order of his own intelligence into the hardware or software of a computer.

This conclusion too is a very "thin slice" of the God of theism. But it's something.

And I think it has to include will as well as mind, because its effects—us, human persons—include will.

The moral argument comes in two forms. The old form, the classical form, starts with the premise of a natural moral law, which every society in history assumed in some form until our present post-Christian society in Western Europe and North America. And if there is a law, there must be a lawgiver behind it. A very clear and simple form of this argument is in book 1 of C. S. Lewis's *Mere Christianity*. It also includes simple and clear answers to objections to the natural law. So does my book *A Refutation of Moral Relativism*, and the last dialogue in *The Best Things in Life*. I also recommend J. Budziszewski's *What We Can't Not Know* if you want an excellent psychological account of the natural law.

The more modern form, formulated first, I think, by Newman, does not assume a natural law but only the authority of individual conscience. Even moral relativists will admit that it is always morally wrong to deliberately disobey your personal conscience, to do what your conscience forbids as morally wrong, whatever it is. Nobody admires a person who deliberately violates his or her own conscience. Now where did conscience get that kind of absolute authority? Not from parents, or society, or evolution, or consensus, or anything else that is questionable and fallible. Why treat these things as if they are the prophets of an infallible God? Only an infallibly right, morally perfect God could have that kind of rightful authority, and only if conscience is his created prophet in the soul are we justified in obeying conscience as if it were that.

This argument is dangerous because it might lead someone to say: "Right; God and conscience are a package deal. Therefore, since I want to deny God more than I want to affirm conscience, instead of accepting both I will deny both. To deny God, I will deny conscience. Raskalnikov, here I come." And we all know what happened to Raskalnikov, don't we? (Have you read *Crime and Punishment?*) Conscience takes its revenge. And on Nietzsche too, poor martyr. In order to kill God he had to kill his own soul. Just what you would expect if the soul is God's image: the image and the original go together. The image can't long survive the death of the original.

If there is no God, we human persons were not created in the image of God but evolved accidentally from mere matter. We are not King God's kids but King Kong's kids. Why then do we have inherent dignity and value? Many atheists bite the bullet and say that's so: nothing has inherent, absolute value because there is no absolute being; there can be no moral absolutism without ontological absolutism, without an ontological ground. I think you as a humanist would not say that. But why not?

Another version of the argument is that if there is no divine providence and no last judgment, no God to tie up all the loose, unjust threads of human history somehow, then *we* have to play God, we have to take Sauron's ring and tidy up Middle-earth. If there's no God, we have to play God and get good results in whatever way works. The end justifies the means. There are no moral absolutes; we may kill or lie or torture if that's the only way to get a better result in the end. Only if there is an all-wise and all-good and all-powerful God writing the story of human history can we say that our job is to obey the absolute commandments God gave us and let the resulting chips fall where they may, even if those chips, those consequences, would be bad, because God will pick up the pieces. The justification for framing an innocent man, for torture, for Hiroshima, for "Sophie's choice" (Have you seen that movie?) is utilitarianism, or consequentialism: the end justifies the means—if there is no God. If He does not exist and command us to obey His laws always and promise to take care of the consequences, then we have to take care of the consequences. So atheism naturally leads to pragmatism, utilitarianism, relativism.

I would not use this argument on any atheist except one like you, who strongly insists on the natural moral law. For one who does not might say not "How foolish my atheistic premise is" but "How necessary the conclusion of moral relativism is once I insist on my atheistic premise."

Your friend,

Peter

31

Dear Michael,

So you see both versions of my moral argument as non sequiturs. You admit the premises but say they do not prove the conclusion. Formally, logically, they do, in both arguments. Perhaps the reason you see the conclusion as a non sequitur is that you read too much into the word "God." You think (probably only subconsciously, since I explicitly repudiated this thought) that the arguments claim to prove the existence of the God of the Bible rather than just a very "thin slice" of Him.

You are also right in saying that my very brief summaries of the two versions of the moral argument are so sketchy that I can hardly expect anyone to be convinced by them. Their sketchiness is one reason; another is that the strength of the moral premise has to be acknowledged by the whole person, including will and feelings and conscience and actions—one's whole life, really—as well as by the rational mind; and the strength of the conclusion is dependent on the strength of the premise.

This does *not* mean that all who disagree with the moral argument for God are immoral, or less moral than those who do. You are rightly suspicious that an argument may have or imply "not only a hidden premise but a hidden agenda, a threatening personal judgment"; and in the hands of some who use this argument, that hidden agenda may really be there. Please be assured that it is not there with me. Not only do I know you only from your letters, so I would be in a poor and perilous position to judge even if I wanted to, but I am under strict orders from my Lord to "judge not, that you be not judged." Judging persons, motives, and hearts is God's prerogative, not man's. (And if there is no God, then either we must judge what we cannot know, or else the most important objects to judge can never be judged. Is that another good moral argument for God?) So even if you are a secret sadist, neo-Nazi, and cannibal, your arguments still deserve a respectful treatment. There's a great line in the play and movie *A Man for All Seasons* (Have you seen it? It's my favorite.) about giving even the devil his due for justice's sake—and therefore also for safety's sake.

Unlike most atheists I know of, you strongly affirm the natural law premise as well as the conscience premise; you just deny "that they constitute a package deal with God." But you don't explain why. You just "sense" how "loose" the connection is. I have no problems with using the intuitive "sense" (in fact, I think that's been sadly neglected in modern philosophy and modern life), but in debate we have to support our intuitions with logical argument. *Why* is the connection between law and lawgiver "loose"? Why doesn't a moral law demand a moral lawgiver behind it, and why doesn't the absolute authority of conscience entail the absolute authority of God behind it? If there is nothing but you behind your conscience, how can *you* have any absolute authority?

And how can you have an absolute duty or obligation to yourself? Duty is an asymmetrical relationship: if x has a duty or obligation to y, y is superior to x. They are not interchangeable in one and the same relationship. But the self is one person, not two. So when we speak of our "duties to ourselves," I think we must mean either our duties to others or to the common good, or else we are covertly thinking of our duties to God but trying to keep God out of the picture, so we substitute ourselves for Him. We sense the absoluteness of the duty much more clearly than we know the ultimate object of it (God), so we misplace the object.

The "personhood" argument does indeed "blend into the mind argument," as you say—or vice versa. But it's richer. A mind is only one power of a person. But yes, the "personhood argument" is relatively new (since "personalism" as an explicit philosophy is only about a century old), and it is more obscure than the argument from mind or the argument from morality. But it's deeper or broader because its premise is our personhood, of which our minds and moralities are only dimensions.

Are you ready to go on to the last three arguments on the list now?

Your friend,
Peter

32

Dear Michael,

We think freely. Our agenda is flexible. Since no one but us is steering the wheel of our minds to the questions on our agenda, we can come back to any of these arguments if we want to if, as you say, "the wind should change or the air should clear up a bit" in your mind or in mine. So let's go on to look at three instances of what I call scientific or historical arguments, arguments from events that actually have happened: miracles, the big bang, and the evolution of mankind, which seems to involve the anthropic principle, which I think is the strongest version of the old "argument from design."

The argument from miracles is the simplest and the most concrete. Of course, atheists deny that miracles have ever happened, since the existence of miracles would prove the existence of a miracle worker, and since a miracle is by definition an event that can't be caused merely by a natural cause, a real miracle would prove the existence of a real supernatural cause—and that certainly is a pretty thick "slice" of God, thicker even than the other cosmological arguments that prove only the distant God of deism. So the whole question here is whether miracles have actually happened. Atheists don't deny the big bang or the anthropic principle, but they do deny miracles.

Unfortunately, we can't go into the historical question here—whether miracles have actually happened—because it's too multifariously detailed. But if I were a tough-minded scientific atheist, that would be my serious research project. I'd go to Mexico City and interview the scientists who tested the tilma of Juan Diego that has resisted decomposition for centuries. (Do you know the story of Guadalupe?) I'd demand chemical analysis of the blood of St. Januarius that is supposed to miraculously liquefy spontaneously, in a public square, on schedule, on his feast day. And so on. I've actually seen one miracle myself, I think. My daughter's brain tumor totally changed from one kind of tumor (a malignant medulla blastoma) to another kind (a benign juvenile astrocytoma) between the CAT scan and the operation. (I wrote about it in the appendix to *Love Is Stronger Than Death*.)

If you want to explore not the historical details about particular miracles but the philosophical and theological question of the *possibility* of miracles as well as the *significance* of miracles, C. S. Lewis's book *Miracles* is your best bet.

Of all miracles, Christ's resurrection is the most important for Christians, because without it, Christianity is dead in the water, for Christ himself is dead. It is the most famous and the most widely believed miracle in history. And for good *reasons*. It is surprisingly defensible. A good debate between an atheist and a theist about that is a book by Antony Flew (when he was still an atheist) and Gary Habermas. It's called *Resurrected? An Atheist and Theist Dialogue*. I think as a scientist you would find the details fascinating and challenging—certainly more concrete, and perhaps more convincing, than our more abstract philosophical arguments. There's a lot of data to be evaluated.

Do you want to go more into the question of miracles in general or the Resurrection in particular next? Or do you want to go into the other two arguments—do you want to tell me in your next letter how you explain the big bang without a big banger and how you explain the universe's detailed "plot" to evolve mankind without seeing divine fingerprints all over the machine?

Your friend,

Peter

33

Dear Michael,

Please don't apologize for not writing. Only a Canadian would apologize for almost being killed by a drunk driver in an accident.

Are you a Canadian, by the way? If so, I assume you're too polite to be insulted by the question. I find that Canadians are so polite that they apologize for apologizing. I have this fantasy where Canadian scientists sneak off to New York City to do their science, because when you do science you have to be no-nonsense, tough-minded, and confrontational.

Three broken ribs, a cracked collarbone, and a concussion, in the hospital for a day and in a neck brace for a month or two—I think that qualifies as a pretty good reason for not writing! Thank God you weren't killed.

Oh, sorry. I forgot. You can't do that, can you, if there is no God to thank?

That was a low blow, I know, but I couldn't resist the temptation. Seriously, it must be tough not to have anyone to thank when you escape something that scary and that close, especially when your doctor used the M-word ("It's a miracle you weren't killed").

So since your brief note just explains your "delinquency" and doesn't offer more arguments of your own but invites me to offer more of mine, "especially about what you so surprisingly say is the most well-attested miracle in history, the reanimation of a corpse two thousand years ago," I accept your invitation to "show me how you can call this an event that is believed 'for good reasons' and with 'surprisingly concrete evidence.'"

I begin with the undeniable empirical data. This consists of two things. The first is the present existence of the Christian Church, with a two-thousand-year-long memory, that is, with its continuously preached and continuously believed message, centering on what it calls the "Gospel" or "good news," which is *not* that God exists and wants us to love each other—that's good but it's hardly news—but that a man who claimed to be God incarnate was crucified and rose from the dead. The second is the existence of the book we call the New Testament, which includes four accounts of this man's life, death, and resurrection, two of which claim to have been written by eyewitnesses and the other two by people who interviewed eyewitnesses, and also letters by Paul of Tarsus, history's most famous and influential missionary, who spread this "good news" around the Mediterranean world until he was martyred in Rome some time in the sixties of the first century AD. That's not belief or hypothesis; that's data.

I claim that a real resurrection (the "hypothesis" of Christianity) is the most rational explanation of the data.

No one doubts that Jesus existed. If he didn't, if he was an invented fictional character, then two fishermen, a tax collector, and a doctor (or if not them, four writers who pretended to be them) invented the most compelling fictional character in history and wrote four different fantasy fiction stories about him that are more brilliant and popular than any other fiction ever written, even Tolkien or Harry Potter—so brilliant that they lastingly convinced billions of intelligent people that they weren't fiction at all (something no other fantasy writer has ever done). The inventors of this story thus perpetuated the biggest hoax, the biggest lie, in the history of the world—and then they died for it, as martyrs, after being hated, misunderstood, excommunicated, imprisoned, tortured, and then beheaded or crucified for not repudiating their hoax. Is that psychologically likely? Do liars die for their lies? Do jokers die for their jokes?

If there was a real Jesus but he never claimed to be God, never performed miracles, and never rose from the dead, then everything interesting in the story is only a fictional invention; then even though the main *character* was not a fiction, the *story* was, especially the miracles, the claim to be God, and the resurrection, which are the most interesting dimensions of the story, the ones that set him apart from everyone else who ever lived. *Somebody* invented the story; stories don't just happen.

The later you put the invention of what we now call the Christian religion, or the Gospel, the harder it is to explain, because the more inventers you have to invent to collaborate on making it up. Has there ever been a great work of fiction written by more than one person? The Arabs say a camel is a horse invented by a committee. Jesus is not a camel.

Who invented Christianity, then? If Jesus invented it, as the Gospels say, we have to explain only one strange man; if the four Gospel writers, four; if his twelve apostles, twelve; if "the early church," thousands.

The texts stand up well to scientific, historical, and literary criticism. Better than any other ancient texts. What other figure do we have four accounts of, from four different authors with four different personalities and to four different audiences and for four different purposes? Matthew writes to Jews to show that Jesus fulfills the Jewish prophecies; Mark writes to action-oriented Romans, emphasizing Jesus getting things done practically; Luke writes to Greeks, in good Greek, and as a doctor emphasizes His healings; and John writes to the whole world, at a later time and in a more philosophical and cosmopolitan way. So we can cross-check; and the cross-checks come out very well indeed, with only the kind of minor discrepancies one would expect of different eye-witnesses (e.g., concerning how many angels and how many women were at the empty tomb on Easter morning, and how Judas died), but with no substantive contradictions between them. Notice I'm appealing only to science, not faith: to history and textual criticism and commonsense psychology.

If the central claim, and the most startling claim—that Jesus literally, physically rose from the grave—is not true, then there are only four other possibilities, logically (if we've eliminated his simple nonexistence). Either he was not crucified; or he was crucified but didn't die; or he died and didn't rise but his disciples lied when they said he did; or he died and didn't rise but his disciples thought he did—they hallucinated.

Let's add a fifth possibility, which is halfway between a lie and a hallucination: the disciples invented a *myth* to make the world believe in Jesus and become more moral and more happy because of this myth—as grown-ups invented the Santa Claus myth to make kids more moral and more happy at Christmas. They didn't mean a literal resurrection but a symbol, or a parable, an allegory.

So either (1) Jesus never existed; or (2) Jesus existed but was never crucified; or (3) Jesus was crucified but survived; or (4) Jesus died and didn't rise, and his disciples lied when they said he rose; or (5) Jesus died and didn't rise, and his disciples hallucinated when they sincerely thought he rose; or (6) Jesus died and didn't rise, and his disciples invented the story of his resurrection as a myth; or (7) Jesus existed, was crucified, died, and rose—in other words, Christianity is true. For if he really rose, that proves he's God, as he says; and that's the fundamental distinctive claim of Christianity. (And, of course, if Jesus is God, then there is indeed a God and atheism is false.)

We refuted (1) already; and no serious scholar believes it anyway.

If (2) is true, all Christians, beginning with Jesus's disciples, either lied, or made an honest mistake, or hallucinated when they said he was crucified. A collective hallucination of a crucifixion is quite incredible. A sincere mistake about who got crucified is only slightly less incredible. They knew him too well to make that mistake. And if they did, all he has to do to dispel it is appear to them and show them his uncrucified body. Also, the Roman and Jewish powers that be that wanted him crucified had to be certain they got the right man. (Both Jewish and Roman law were very strict about such things. These people were not barbarians.)

So it's got to be a lie. But if the crucifixion is a lie, it's got to be part of the lie that is the whole story of crucifixion and resurrection—you have to have a corpse in order to have a resurrection—so (2), the no-crucifixion theory, collapses into (4), the lie theory.

(3) Could he have been crucified but survived? No. No one survives a crucifixion. Roman law demanded medical proof of death. John used a legal formula for an eyewitness when he wrote that he saw water as well as blood come out when the centurion

pierced Jesus's side with a lance (Jn 19:31–37). That "water" (or body fluid) came from the lungs, which had collapsed and had asphyxiated him; that's why they didn't have to break his legs and induce asphyxiation by hanging, as they did to the two thieves who were crucified with him and were still alive when the Romans checked. (They had to get the bodies down before sunset, which began the Jewish Sabbath day, because the Jews would have rioted if the Romans had desecrated their sacred time.)

If he *had* survived the crucifixion, in something like a catalyptic fit or catatonic trance, and was buried in the tomb because he seemed to be dead, how could he have gotten out? They put a great stone over the door of the tomb. It took at least two strong men to move it. How could a man who had just been whipped and crucified roll away the stone? How could he have overpowered the Roman guards who were placed at the tomb to stop the disciples from stealing the body (Mt 27:62–66)? How could he have convinced his disciples who saw him on Sunday (the third day) that he was not a semicorpse badly in need of medical treatment but the victorious, divine lord of life and death?

The lie theory, (4), is the most natural and reasonable alternative to a real resurrection and the earliest one. It's mentioned in the Gospels (Mt 28:11–15). The biggest problem with that is that no Christian ever confessed the "lie." They all risked death or actually died for it. (Both the Jews and the Romans desperately wanted to quash this rebellious new movement.) Martyrdom doesn't prove truth, but it certainly proves sincerity. Who would die for a lie?

And if he really stayed dead and the resurrection is a lie, where is the body? All the ruling authorities, both the Jews and the Romans, wanted to nip this movement in the bud, and the public display of Jesus's corpse would have done that defifnitively. So where's the body? The disciples must have stolen it. But how did they overpower the armed Roman guards? And who moved the stone? (Frank Morrison's little classic by that title (*Who Moved the Stone?*) has been in print for almost one hundred years.) And above all, why did they die for their lie?

(5) Suppose they were not deceivers but deceived. Hallucinations happen, and occasionally even collectively. But not for forty days (Acts 1:3) and on many different occasions (compare the last chapters of the four Gospels). Hallucinations don't eat (Lk 24:36–43), cook (Jn 21:1–14), or let themselves be touched (Jn 20:24–29). If that did not happen, the disciples invented it, and then we are brought back to the "lie" theory.

(6) Why couldn't the story be a myth? Pagan myths often include dying and rising gods. The pagans had myths or fables, but the Jews did not. And even if these twelve Jews suddenly became pagans and embraced this repudiated and foreign thought form, their leader (Peter) explicitly denied that it was a myth (2 Pt 1:16). Once kiddie asks Mommy whether Santa is myth or fact, Mommy lies when she says he is fact and *not* myth. So the "myth" theory also collapses into the "lie" theory.

(7) So what else is there? Christianity, the most widely believed religion in the world. The reasons for it come from the data. The only reasons against it come from ideological prejudices and philosophical presuppositions (atheism, naturalism, scientism, materialism).

It may not be a mathematically tight "proof"—that's what you get in math, not in history—but it's certainly a strong argument based on specific evidence. You asked for it, so here it is.

Your friend,

Peter

34

Dear Michael,

I'm no more trained in history than you are. But we both know common sense, logic, and the science of using evidence. I didn't expect you to come up with some clear, sharp new answer to these traditional arguments, an answer that all unbelievers from now on would quote. Nor did I expect a sudden change of mind and a religious conversion. So let's leave that argument on the back burner and turn to the two other arguments from facts, from history and science, beginning with the big bang (i.e., beginning with the beginning!).

As I understand it (correct me if I have this wrong), if we combine Einstein's relativity with big bang cosmology, we get the conclusion that time itself is only 14.7 billion years old. For time is relative to matter (and space), and all matter began 14.7 billion years ago. There is no time before the big bang, that is, no time before the beginning of all time, any more than there is any space outside the universe, which is the sum of all spatial, material entities, time, and space being not Newtonian absolutes but relativities that do not preexist matter. Matter (mass) even curves space, and its movement, if fast enough, "curves" time (the "twin paradox").

Before the big bang was empirically and mathematically proved, all physicists who were atheists called it creationism in disguise. For it matches the biblical account of creation, unlike both the steady state theory or the eternal oscillating universe theory, the "accordion" theory, with bangs and crushes occurring in unending alteration. But big bang is true, and science has proved it in many ways.

So what caused it? To maintain atheism in the face of big bang, you have to give up the principle of causality itself, at least for the universe as a whole. You have to say that large blue rabbits don't just happen for no reason at all, yet universes do. That sounds absolutely crazy. To avoid any kind of God (a big banger), you abandon the most fundamental principle of all science, all common sense, and all philosophy, namely the principle of causality, the principle that whatever happens has a reason why it happens, a cause. How open-minded is *that*? I think it takes a genius like Stephen Hawking to take that seriously. We have a saying in academia: "That idea is so crazy that only a PhD could possibly believe it." Sure, it's *mathematically* possible, or calculable. But to quote another commonsense proverb, "Figures don't lie, but liars figure." Another one says, "There are three kinds of lies: lies, damned lies, and statistics."

I'm not saying that the big bang proves that the banger is the God of the Bible, the personal creator. For the scientific evidence does not reach back beyond that event, since that event is the beginning of the universe and all scientific evidence is "inside" the universe. (The "inside" is meant ontologically, not spatially, of course, since there can be no space or place "outside" the universe that contains, or is, all of space.)

But we can reason logically, by good philosophy, to something "outside" the universe (or rather "transcendent to" the universe, more than the universe) in two ways: first, that it must exist, since every event needs a cause, and secondly, that its nature must be nonmaterial, nonspatial, and nontemporal, since all matter, space, and time is "in" the universe. But immateriality and eternity (timelessness) are divine attributes. So even though this argument doesn't bring us to the God of the Bible, it certainly seems to give us a pretty "thick slice" of Him, even though the "slice" is only negative (nonmaterial, nonspatial, nontemporal).

So what do you do with the big bang?

Your friend,

Peter

35

Dear Michael,

For the first time, you've stumped me: I don't understand most of the math in your letter. I never took a course in statistics or probability theory or in the speculative dimensions of higher math, nor have I made a point of remedying this gap in my education.

But common sense tells me there can be no way to calculate the probability of an "absolute singularity" or of alternatives to it. Is there? If so, can you explain it in dummy terms? Does higher math just leave common sense behind entirely?

Nor do I understand the alternative scenario of a "multiverse" (many universes). Are they merely *possible* universes? Of course they are possible: talking trees or four-headed fish or flying monkeys could have evolved. Anything not logically contradictory is possible. If you say that these many universes are not only possible but also actual, why do you say this? What possible evidence could you have for their actual existence? You can't answer merely that mathematics can calculate their possibilities or compossibilities. Geneticists can probably calculate the possibility of the evolution of flying monkeys, given all the other environmental factors millions of years ago, but that's because they have data within this universe for the possibility or probability of other things in it. But how can we have data for another universe, since "another universe" means "another universe *of* data"?

I see no reason for assuming that everything that is logically and mathematically possible is also actual. But I see good reason for assuming that everything actual has at least two causes: an actual efficient cause and a formal cause or formula that makes it logically possible (in contrast to square circles, e.g.). In this universe, the only actual universe we know, we have nonflying monkeys rather than flying monkeys or no monkeys because of certain evolutionary efficient causes. Why do we have this universe, then? Its formal cause makes it logically possible, but what is its efficient cause? There must be an efficient cause to actualize its inherent possibility, its formal cause, as there is an evolutionary cause that actualized horses but not unicorns. Thus we are back to the big banger.

And if you say that a "previous" universe caused this one, you are extending time beyond the bounds of this universe. "Previous" in what time scheme? Isn't that the old Newtonian fallacy of absolute time? Aren't you throwing Einstein under the Newtonian bus?

Perhaps we are just not meeting each other's arguments at all here, for I am arguing on a logical, commonsensical, philosophical level, a "prescientific" level, if you will; while you are arguing on a mathematical and strictly scientific level. If you have failed to instruct me in the mysteries of your "level," that is probably the fault of my education. But if I have failed to engage you on my commonsensical level, that cannot be the fault of your education, since common sense is common, that is, universal, and thus precedes education, rather than being education specific. I don't know whether I'm insulting myself or you the most here, but I think I can plead ignorance while you cannot.

If you have some device for breaking up our logjam here, please try. Otherwise, I think we should go on to the argument from design and the anthropic principle. I don't see any reason why we will get into another logjam there, since the mathematics involved is only simple probability theory—for example, multiplying the probabilities (or improbabilities) of events by each other to calculate the probability of a collective event—which I think I do understand. All the calculations I have read of the probability of mankind evolving anywhere in the universe (assuming trillions or even quadrillions of planets) are in the range of the mind boggling. I remember one figure: it was 1 in 10 to the 183rd power.

You know the details: if the temperature of the universe a few seconds after the big bang had been a millionth of a degree hotter or colder, no carbon molecules (the basis of all life) could ever have evolved. The possibility of hydrogen and oxygen combining into water is almost as unlikely. If any of the conditions of heat, pressure, mass, and so on had been the tiniest part different, no protein molecules could have evolved. If the moon had been nonexistent, or multiple, or much bigger or smaller, we'd have no regular tides, which are needed to evolve amphibians and thus mammals. I probably got some of the details wrong, but they are so numerous that I can presume you know some of them too. If anything looks like the result of a plot rather than an accident, it's ourselves. It's like a million windows in an enormous maze opening just enough and just at the right time for a bird to escape through them. And these are the windows of opportunity for human evolution.

I've never understood why Christians (almost always Protestants, for some reason I can't figure out) feel instinctively threatened by evolution, both cosmic and chemical and biological. To me, it provides the most compelling data for design. And by all analogies, design means a designer, an intelligence before, and not just after, the process of evolution. Would anyone say a supercomputer, or New York City, or the *Last Supper* had appeared just by blind, random chance? Does anyone explain the dialogues of Plato by an explosion in a print factory? (And even if so, you first have to have the print factory.) Why then do atheists scramble to find alternative explanations to a divine designer for the most complex thing in the universe, ourselves, as a biological species with a brain and nervous system cybernetically complex enough to host rational thought? The answer seems psychologically obvious. It does not look like an open-minded, unprejudiced search for truth. Can you show me why it is?

Your friend,
Peter

36

Dear Michael,

Your answer to my last question seems to be to be nothing but a tautology: you say that if the universe had not evolved rational creatures like us, there would be no rational creatures and thus no reasoning about the universe. In other words, only a universe with persons in it can be the object of science and manifest what is called the "anthropic principle." Well, duh! We can wonder why we're here only because we're here. Is that supposed to be an *explanation*?

You try to turn the anthropic principle on its head and make it out to be evidence *against* divine design, or at least against all possible *argument for* divine design, when you say that "the anthropic principle shows *not* that there is a God who chose this universe rather than others, as a man chooses a fertile woman rather than an infertile one because he wants children" (a very good image, by the way!), "but merely that it is impossible for us to imagine any alternative universe that does not produce human life and reason."

A sidebar here: you are assuming, and I am denying your assumption, that *reason* is produced merely by the material universe, as monkeys and brains are.

It's true, of course, that it's impossible for us to imagine another universe *without* us. That's true because it's a tautology: you can't imagine yourself not existing and therefore not imagining. So your premise is true.

But that does not mean that this universe of ours in which we exist is *the only possible universe*. There are quintillions of other perfectly possible and consistent alternative universes that would not have evolved any human life.

This is known not just by science but by commonsense logic. See Leibnitz's "possible worlds" theory: it seems simple and self-evident to me. Is it not so to you?

I also do not claim that God is the only possible answer to the question you formulated: "What chose this universe out of all possible universes to actualize? Was it God or something else? And was it a choice or something else?" That's not part of the argument. Again you seem to be wrongly assuming that I'm trying to prove the God of the Bible. I don't start with this "thick," revealed God and then try to prove Him; I just start with the natural evidence and then try to explain it rationally. It's you who, I think, are beginning with the biblical notion of God and desperately trying to avoid Him. I'm dealing, in my conclusion, with only the "thin slice" of God; you're dealing with the "thick God" in your prior demand to justify your disbelief in that "thick" God; and therefore, you see even my "thin slices" as threatening. Ask yourself honestly whether my amateur psychologizing isn't really on target here.

I'm not trying to win the logical argument psychologically; that's a fallacy. I'm trying to keep both of us out of the personal, psychological, religious dimension while we look at the natural, rational, philosophical, logical, and scientific arguments. I think it's you, not I, who are "sneaking religion into the secular debate."

I say all this only because I trust you not to use my candor as an excuse for dismissing my question as "judgmental." If you detect any similar presuppositions or presumptions in my thought, I would be grateful, not resentful, to be corrected. I tried to be totally candid and honest about my motives in this debate right up front at the beginning.

I'm glad the doctor told you that you might risk removing your neck brace in a few days. But remember, he used the word "risk." And remember how our desires and fears cloud our judgment. That's one reason we pay disinterested doctors to give us advice as well as treatment.

In our attempt to be "disinterested doctors" in the matter of atheism versus theism, we must both remember that our motives are always complex and mixed. There is no question of simply eliminating some of these motives, only of letting the right one, the search for objective truth, prevail over the others, including even the charitable desire to persuade a friend out of an important illusion, and of course the desire for personal victory and self-justification, and (for both of us, in opposite ways) a better, happier, or more comfortable life with or without God. We must both be more, not less, severe on ourselves than I have been on you in questioning your motives.

Your friend,
Peter

37

Dear Michael,

You are probably being overly polite (are you *sure* you're not Canadian?) in saying that you feel "almost as uncertain of the math of the anthropic principle argument" as I do. But I appreciate your candor, and I agree that we are much more likely to reach some understanding on the moral argument, since we are both "moralists." So let's go back to that earlier argument, as we said we might do. (Writing letters is more like reading a book than writing a book: you can skip around as you please.)

Yes, I do believe that "you can't be good without God," and I also believe that there are good atheists, even very good atheists, as well as bad theists, even very bad theists. These two admissions logically entail that even atheists have God in some real way whenever they are good, just as it entails that God is working in them every time they discover truth by reason. The God of theism, as distinct from the gods of pagan polytheism, is the source of all truth and goodness—otherwise, he would not be God, just someone like Zeus. So ontologically there can be no other first cause of any truth, including true goodness, or of any goodness, including the goodness of truth, for a theist. That's a necessary part of the "package deal" of theism. As Arthur Holmes wrote, "All truth is God's truth." As all hobbits are Tolkien's hobbits.

However, that does not mean, as some fundamentalists say, that only believers have a real ontological connection with God or the active presence of God in the soul that explains moral conscience. Fundamentalists don't usually think in ontological terms. They tend to think in psychological and subjective terms. And in those terms, some of them say that no unbeliever has any presence of God in his or her soul, or mind, or heart, or spirit at all. That is not the classical Christian position, and in fact it was officially condemned by at least two ecumenical councils, Vaticans I and II, and by the CCC (Catechism of the Catholic Church), and by the greatest of the church fathers, including Justin Martyr, Clement of Alexandria, John of Damascus, and Augustine. And, of course, Aquinas.

So we're arguing from a piece of data we both share (conscience, or awareness of and obligation to the moral law). I say that God best explains that data. You do not. So once again it's an issue of which of two opposite hypotheses best explains the common data.

I think the moral argument is stronger today than in the past, because to see the full force of the argument you have to envision a real alternative—that morality is merely an undesigned, blind, evolutionary invention for survival—and that alternative was not generally available to the premodern mind. Even the pagans, from Greeks and Romans to American Indians and Australian Aborigines, acknowledged a real moral law. And certainly all religions do.

My claim is that far from casting more doubt on the moral premise of the moral argument for God, modern "immoralism" or "amoralism," with its moral nihilism, or moral relativism, or moral subjectivism, or moral utilitarianism, is really the "existentially" strongest version of the moral argument. It's a *reductio ad absurdum*. For if there is no absolute, eternal, necessary, perfect, nonnegotiable being there as the ultimate ground of moral goodness, then the moral imperative to be good that we feel in our conscience is not based on anything higher than human thinking and desiring, plus the obvious biological fact that when we act morally, with justice and charity and compassion to each other, we survive better and are usually happier than when we bonk each other on the head whenever we feel like it. In that case, why not be a Nietzschean immoralist "superman" if we can get away with it, if we can be bonkers without being bonkees? I see no other possible answer a typical modern can give to that question except: "Because you won't get away with it. Our cops will get you, and our will will prevail over yours." But that's not necessarily true, factually. Even now, criminals get away with more than half of all the crimes they commit. So the question remains: *Why not* be immoral?

And all other answers to the "Why not?" question are weak. "Because the rest of the human race will hate you"? So what, if I don't *want* to be loved by the fools I abuse? "Because you'll feel pangs of conscience"? Not if I successfully perfom a consciencectomy. And that doesn't take a radical Nietzschean leap into superman, it just takes a consistent moral relativism à la *Brave New World* (which is almost no longer a prophecy of the future but an observation of the present among the "educated" masses in Western civilization).

Why is "God" a better answer, then? Not merely or mainly because He, unlike human cops, will infallibly get you in the end, but because He makes being good the very essential nature of ultimate reality. "You must be holy because I the Lord am holy," is the repeated reason He gave for being moral and obeying His laws, to His chosen people, the Jews, His collective prophet to the world. In other words, "Because that's the way it is; that's the way I AM." Sanctity is really sanity: living in conformity with reality.

Let's try a different approach to the same point (that morality proves God). Step one: "moral relativism" is an oxymoron, like "mathematical relativism." Justice and charity can no more change to being evil than two can change to being an odd number. Step two: the human reason and will is an inadequate ultimate basis for this moral absolutism.

Kant tried to deny step two, in his third formulation of the categorical (absolute moral) imperative. He said true morality had to be "autonomous," that is, man-made. Our will, not another will, not even the divine will, had to be the origin of moral law. "Our will" here means not "our selfish, psychological desires and passions" but "our practical moral reason." But even then, the very same person—myself—who is bound by the moral absolutes of the categorical imperative is the one who is doing the binding. If I am the authority by which I am bound, I am also the authority by which I am unbound. If the law comes from me, how can it come *to* me? Each individual human self is one, not two, so that if the self and its will is above the law, as its creator, it cannot at the same time be under it, as duty-bound to it.

Kant tried to solve this problem by distinguishing the "transcendental ego," which subconsciously made the moral law from the conscious "empirical ego" of everyday experience that is bound by it. But this distinction is just theism in pantheistic disguise. The "transcendental ego" was interpreted by his disciples

(Fichte, Schelling, and Hegel) to be a kind of single collective universal pantheistic God, or Hindu Atman. Its ontological *address* was different (not transcendent to the soul but immanent in it, or even *as* it: the "transcendental ego"), but its moral *function* was the same (to be the ultimate source of moral law). Atheists like Schopenhauer and Nietzsche and Sartre saw through this disguise easily. I think you will too.

But if you do, if you reject this inconsistent middle way of Kant and the Enlightenment and are left only with the two alternatives of theism with an absolute morality or atheism without it, you may embrace atheism without it if you are more concerned with atheism than with morality. The eighteenth-century French Enlightenment *philosophes* that Sartre read, who proposed what I've called the Kantian "middle way," only helped convince Sartre to be a consistently atheistic immoralist. He argued, very logically, that "there can be no a priori Good because there is no absolute and eternal consciousness to think it."

If, as I suspect, this argument at least bothers you, since you say you accept a "natural law" moral absolutism, I hope you will at least modify your atheism to an agnosticism like Camus's, who could not clearly see how to reconcile godlessness and moral absolutism. He could not either move from godlessness to religious belief or abandon moral absolutism. Thus the trilemma of the most compelling and admirable character in all his fiction, Dr. Rieux in *The Plague*. He risks his life to save thousands of people from a plague because he knows that "the meaning of life is to be a saint." He also knows that "you can't be a saint without God," and yet he can't believe in God. Camus never solved that trilemma, which was his as well as Dr. Rieux's, because he could never reject any one of those three propositions. Yet he knew that if any two of them are true, the third one must be false. Dr. Rieux sounds a lot like you.

If Camus had lived longer, I think it is at least very likely that this moral pressure, of both logic and conscience, would have led him to accept God. Even some of his atheist or agnostic critics say that.

I hope you will live much longer than Camus did. Please do not drive fast sports cars. And don't do things your doctor calls risky with that neck brace!

Your friend,

Peter

38

Dear Michael,

You're right: you've been defending and I've been attacking all the while; it's time to switch places. I'm not reluctant to do this, because I think it is easier to answer the arguments against theism than to prove theism. The weaknesses I find in the arguments for atheism and in its objections against theism are often quite simple—factual or logical mistakes—while the weaknesses in the arguments for theism and its objections against atheism are typically more complex, subtle, abstract, and philosophical.

You list six objections: (1) hell, (2) the problem of evil, (3) evil theists, (4) the harm religion has allegedly done in history, (5) any absolute religion's tendency to oppress and persecute heretics, and (6) "religion's obsession with sexual morality." You also "reserve the right to trot out many more witnesses for the prosecution" in the future. Fine.

I'm glad you picked on hell first, because that seems to me the hardest of all the Christian beliefs to justify. If I had the authority to eliminate any one Christian doctrine, that is certainly the one I would eliminate. But, then, I'd also eliminate cancer, neo-Nazis, suicide bombers, and bureaucratic red tape throughout the world if I could, but I can't, and the fact that I hate them doesn't mean they don't exist.

So let's go to hell first. It is indeed a nonnegotiable doctrine, though many Christians have tried to negotiate it away. It is non-negotiable not only because the three highest authorities in Christianity all clearly teach it (Christ, the church He founded, and the Bible it canonized and declared to be infallible), but also because it logically follows from admitting the existence of just two things: human free will and God. If we have free will to the end, we have the free will to either accept or reject God in the end. As C. S. Lewis wrote, "There are only two kinds of people, in the end: those who say to God, 'Your will be done' and those to whom God says, '*Your* will be done.'" Same point put differently: God says "Your will be done" to everybody, but only some of us say it back to Him.

As you point out, if there is no God, I cannot argue that the admission of human free will entails the existence of hell. In other words, hell follows not just from free will but only from the combination "There is a God and there is also a free will." (You admit that this is a strong reason for your atheism, since you find it easier to deny God, which you have not experienced, than to deny free will, which you have experienced.)

I said earlier that I probably don't believe in the God you don't believe in either. I say the same about hell: I don't believe in the hell you don't believe in either. For there are at least five mistakes in what seems to me is your picture of hell.

First, hell does not mean that God hates the damned. He loves them, as a good father loves a rebellious child. In fact, some of the saints say that it is the very love of God that tortures the damned in hell. Many of us can remember, from our early and uncivilized years, occasional hell-like states of mind when we were tortured by our parents' love rather than their anger. We just wanted to fight them, because we selfish little egotists thought we had to be totally in the right and they therefore had to be totally in the wrong; but instead of fighting us, they hugged us and told us they loved us. But we didn't want to be hugged or loved! We wanted to fight. Maybe that's a tiny foretaste of hell.

Some of the saints say that heaven and hell may even be the same place, consisting of the same objective reality—the truth and love of God—but experienced in opposite ways. A and B sit together at an opera: for A it's heaven and for B it's hell. Then they both go to a grunge rock concert: it's the reverse, hell for A and heaven for B. Truth—which is what God is—is heaven to honest and good people, but it can be hell and torturing to dishonest and evil people, who "loved darkness rather than light, because their deeds were evil," as a certain great Jewish psychologist once said (Jn 3:19). The same light is good for the bird and bad for the worm. The same dentist is good to the tooth and bad for the cavity.

Your second misunderstanding is that hell does not mean that God throws anyone into it against their will. Ghandi said "God is not Strength but Truth." His judgment is simply truth, light. It shows up what is. And since we have free will, it is possible that what is in us is the fundamental choice against God rather than for Him. I think those who choose hell enter it proudly singing, "I did it my way."

You may ask: How can any sane person possibly choose torture over bliss? Of course no one chooses torture as such or rejects bliss as such. But suppose what we choose between is two compounds rather than elements, two package deals. Suppose we know that the torture is the price we have to pay for some desired evil. We can still commit the evil. We often do just that. "The hell with the consequences; I want what I want." We can choose either way in such complex act-and-consequences "package deals." Even when we know that we may suffer for the rest of our lives, we still sometimes murder, betray, or cheat. It is possible. It happens. We are not rational; we are sometimes morally insane.

Or suppose that we know that the bliss we want entails a pain, a sacrifice. We can still reject that "package deal" even when we admit that the bliss will outweigh the pain.

Suppose, further, that the most important moral evil is selfishness and the most important moral good is unselfish love. Suppose our very nature is designed to find supreme bliss only by unselfishness, by sacrifice of that "I did it my way," and suppose that without sacrificing that egotism it is eternally impossible for us to find our ultimate bliss and satisfaction. In that case, hell would be quite terrifyingly easy to choose.

A third misunderstanding is that hell does not mean that God tortures people there. He does not want their torture. The Bible says that "God is not willing that any should perish." But that which He essentially is and cannot change—truth and unselfish love—may torture them there, because they have made themselves into the kind of persons that do not love these things but hate them. But God can't help that: He can't turn off His love any more than the sun can turn off its light. Thus paradoxically, God's essential, eternal character—truth and love—is both the supreme heavenly foundation for moral goodness and its joyful reward and the thing that tortures the damned in hell, which is the supreme evil and misery.

I admit that this is "the sophisticated, philosophical picture of the doctrine of hell" rather than "the popular picture of most believers." But a *picture* is only an image. Material pictures of spiritual things are not to be mistaken for literal descriptions. That includes the pictures of God in the Bible as a man. It's very clear that He is *not* a man; but "a man" is the closest image we have for Him because He created only us, and no other animal, us "in His image and likeness (distant resemblance)." So my "sophisticated" picture of hell (which is not a picture or material image at all) does not contradict, but only interprets, the concrete, material pictures in the popular (and biblical!) imagination. The Bible, after all, is addressed to the ordinary populace, not to philosophers. And so it gets its essential truth across best by images (especially fire) that terrify most people more than abstract concepts do. (It's also symbolically accurate, since fire *destroys*.) The Bible also gives us pictures of fallen, evil angels, demons or devils, torturing souls in hell. I don't honestly know quite how literally to take those pictures, but Jesus clearly taught that the devil is real. The essential idea of the devil as a great, powerful, and clever evil spirit does not seem ridiculous to me, though the popular (not biblical) pictorial details, the horns and hoofs and red tights and tutus, do. The doctrine seems reasonable: if God created bodiless spirits that are intelligent and free as well as embodied ones (us), then some of them, like some of us, may well have chosen evil over good, self over God. And they rather than God may have invented hell. I do not stand firm in interpreting these things, which are beyond our experience.

I think that also takes care of your fourth point: hell does not mean that God made it or "invented" it. God is good. Hell is evil.

Whatever invented hell is evil. And, therefore, that "whatever" must be something in evil spirits, or in us, not in God.

Here is a fifth misunderstanding. You say, quite eloquently, "When we contemplate the idea of hell, we find that it is a place that contains people like Uncle Harry, a violent and selfish man but still a man, and therefore with some good in him as well as much evil. He is supposedly in hell for just punishment: to pay for his temporal and temporary sins by eternally suffering a far greater pain and torture than he ever experienced for a single second in his life. It is as if Dr. Mengele, with snide Nazi sneers, was there, torturing and twisting and pricking and burning his most sensitive body parts and gleefully hearing his insane, panic-filled screams 24/7. And this is called justice?"

What's wrong with this picture is (1) that hell's tortures are spiritual, not physical, and (2) that what is in hell is not Uncle Harry but ex-Harry; not a person like us in our present condition, inner as well as outer, with torture added. It is an ex-person, one who has lost the very ability to say "I." (Thus in the Gospels, when Jesus asks the demon-possessed man his name, he replies, "Our name is Legion, for we are many.") This thing is to a human being what ashes are to a house. It is an ex-human being. It has lost its soul, its identity, its personhood, its unity, its nature, its *logos*, its reason for being. It has made an ash of itself.

This "sophisticated picture" is not less terrible than the popular picture of retaining your human identity and being tortured; it is more terrible, because it means losing the very greatest and best thing in us, which is not pleasure and freedom from pain and torture but selfhood, the image of God, the God who revealed His name to Moses in the burning bush as "*I* AM." "I" is the name for a person.

I do not insist on this interpretation of hell, although I think it is both reasonable and orthodox. These are mysterious matters, and I do not expect you to suddenly understand and agree. All I claim to have done is to have answered your objections, not adequately enough to satisfy the mind's desire to know all the answers, but adequately enough to have loosened the link between your premise (that Christianity teaches hell) and your conclusion (that the Christian God does not exist). Like the problem of evil in general, hell is indeed apparent evidence against God. But it is not definitive and unimpeachable evidence.

Unless you think you have a really important, clear, and knock-'em-down-drag-'em-out argument against what I've said (in which case let's not omit it), let's move to objection 2, okay?

Your friend,

Peter

39

Dear Michael,

There are many formulations of the "problem of evil" as an argument against God's existence. The simplest one is this is: "If God, no evil; evil, therefore no God." Your version fleshes out the reason for the first premise ("If God, no evil"). It's very well put; I quote you word for word, adding only numbers for reference:

(1) If God exists, he is all good, all wise, and all powerful. (A being lacking any one of these attributes is not what Christians mean by "God.")

(2) (2A) If he is all good, he wills only good, everywhere, to all his creatures;

(3) (2B) And if he is all wise, he knows perfectly what is for his creatures' good.

(4) (2C) And if he is all powerful, he gets exactly what he wills.

(5) Therefore if God exists, he would be (3A) good enough to want only good, not evil, (3B) wise enough to know how to get it, and (3C) powerful enough to be able to get it.

(6) So if God exists, there would be no evil.

(7) But evil exists.

(8) Therefore God lacks either goodness, wisdom, power, or existence itself. If he exists, he is either evil, stupid, or weak. He either *wants* evil, or doesn't *know* how to avoid it, or *can't* avoid it.

(9) But if God is either evil, stupid, or weak, then God (at least the Christian God) does not exist. (This is a corollary of point (1).)

(10) Therefore, (the Christian) God does not exist.

The problem of evil is surely the strongest argument for atheism in the history of human thought. The simplest answer to it is that in a sense God, though omnipotent, can't avoid human evil. He can avoid evil in himself and in all beings that he creates without free will, but not in a created being who has real free will, that is, the real ability to choose either good *or evil*. The laws of logic make it impossible for even an omnipotent being to at the same time create creatures with real free will *and* infallibly necessitate that no evil is ever chosen. God can do all things, but a logical self-contradiction is not a thing, a meaningful thing, at all. A set of words that contradicts itself and thus says nothing with any intelligible meaning at all does not suddenly become meaningful when you add the words "God can" to it.

So God can either (a) not create any beings with free will, in which case there would indeed be no evil, or (b) create beings with free will, in which case it is up to them, not God, whether evil exists or not.

Would you really rather God had chosen (a) rather than (b)?

This directly explains moral evil, or sin. It does not directly explain physical evil, or suffering, disease, death, and imperfection. Though that is not the worst kind of evil, it is the hardest to explain, to reconcile with a perfect God. These nonmoral evils must be due either to (1) the inherent and necessary weakness and limitations of finite beings (in which case the only way God could have avoided all evil, even these nonmoral evils, would have been not to create anything at all) or to (2) the results of human (and perhaps also angelic) moral and spiritual evil. That is what the Genesis story seems to teach, though the causal mechanism that brings about the effect (physical evils) from the cause (moral evil) is not explained. In the story in Genesis, there was no physical evil (death, suffering, pain) for man until there was moral and spiritual evil (sin). So we are responsible for all evil: moral evils directly and physical evils indirectly.

But how can our sin be responsible for physical evils? Here is one possible answer. Perhaps the psychosomatic unity we had before the Fall was much greater than what we have now, so that when pre-fallen Adam broke his leg climbing a mountain he just smiled, said, "Oops," and psychosomatically healed himself. When the soul is in perfect harmony with God, the body and nature should be in perfect harmony with the soul; when the soul rebels against God, the body and nature rebel against the soul. When the prime minister leaves the employ and authority of the king, his secretary no longer gets paid, because the chain of authority has been broken. All good trickles down from God; once that path is blocked, its lower reaches then can experience alternatives to good.

I do not insist on that explanation, though it seems reasonable to me—at least reasonable enough to declaw your objection.

Finally, you ask the question "Why can't God, if he infallibly foresees everything, create only those people he foresees will choose to go to heaven and just not create the people he foresees will choose to go to hell?—assuming that infallible foreknowledge and free will are not logically incompatible, which is another problem."

My first answer, the one I'm most confident of, is that I just don't know for sure.

My second answer is that people influence each other in all sorts of indirect, interdependent ways, so what you are asking God to do is logically impossible, I think. You're thinking of people as autonomous, separate entities; they're not. They're conditioned, even in their good and evil choices, by each other and each other's choices, by their life stories, their families, their interactions. Those choices are *conditioned* (influenced) even though not *determined* (necessitated).

My third answer is that the apparent contradiction between infallible foreknowledge and free will was solved long ago by Boethius in chapter 5 of *The Consolation of Philosophy*: God doesn't literally foresee because He's not in time. What is past or future to us is present to God. He is the eternal contemporary of everything that ever happens, including our free choices. To see and know a free choice happening in the present moment when it's happening does not remove the freedom of the choice, even if the knowledge is infallible.

But this is a very complex and obscure question, especially my second answer. Of course, just because I don't know an answer, that doesn't mean there isn't one.

By the way, if we *didn't* bump up against unanswerable puzzles, we'd have a right to suspect we were dealing with something we made up rather than with reality. The analogy with science is quite close: when we deal with the real world, we are not dealing with a Crystal Palace but with a cave. We see only a little and often bump our head on surprises. This applies to the real world of spirit as well as the real world of matter.

That analogy with science also helps answer the problem of evil. If we had all the answers to this most mysterious problem, we'd be God, and there'd be no need for a superior being. So the fact that the problem of evil counts against God counts for God. It's consistent with the God hypothesis. If there *were* a God whose wisdom was as superior to ours as ours is to a flea's, we would find exactly what we do find when we explore the caves that He invented: darkness, mysteries. He alone has X-ray vision. So the evidence against the God hypothesis, namely the problem of evil, is evidence for it, or at least is consistent with it.

Your friend,

Peter

40

Dear Michael,

Really, now, I shouldn't deserve such fulsome praise for being ignorant of the best answer to your excellent question and honestly confessing this ignorance. Is that honesty really so rare among your friends? I don't think it is among mine. (Notice that since we are each other's friends, it's tricky to make out whether that's a hidden insult or a hidden compliment! It's like Bilbo's farewell at his birthday party: "I don't like half of you half as much as you deserve"—or something like that.)

Now that we're out of hell, we can consider your next objection to theism. (I don't think they can have conversations like this in hell!) This is not just the problem of evil in general but the problem of evil believers. And this too does indeed count, and count very strongly, against theism. Chesterton once said that the only really strong argument against Christianity was Christians.

One answer is that it's equally true that the really strong argument for Christianity is Christians: wise and good ones, joyful and saintly ones.

But, you object, if God is perfect and faith is not just an intellectual opinion but a personal relationship of trust, and if God comes into believers' lives when they ask Him to, and if Christians want to be saints, why doesn't God make them all saints? That would convert the world pretty effectively.

I congratulate you on formulating the question more fairly and more strongly than unbelievers usually do. You understand what faith is better than many believers do. If faith means letting God in, into our lives and into our very souls, then why doesn't He do a complete job of cleaning us up once we invite Him in?

The two answers are time and free will.

We are creatures of time and gradual changes. And God deals with every creature according to its nature. So He does clean us up, but gradually rather than instantly. And the reason it's so gradual is that we still insist on sinning a lot, even while we consent to being repaired of sin. We hop around on the operating table telling Doctor God how to do the operation and complaining about its pains. And we can do that because we have free will.

But you are right that the sins of believers count against God. In fact, I think they count more heavily than anything else. If a saint is the strongest argument for religion, a sinner is the strongest argument against it. But both are a strange kind of "argument": one whose data we not only *discover* but *make* by our choices. So the most effective way to argue for religious faith, the most effective way to convert unbelievers and win the world, is to be a saint. It worked: saints converted the hard-nosed Roman Empire. Mother Teresa is probably responsible for a thousand times more conversions than the best writer, apologist, "intellectual," or theologian of the twentieth century, whoever that is. (I'd say it's either G. K. Chesterton or C. S. Lewis.)

Finally, to complain that there are so many sinners in the church is like complaining that there are so many sick people in the hospital.

I really don't know what more to say about this objection, so I'll just stop here, even though this letter is short. Size is less important than we think in almost every field.

Your friend,

Peter

41

Dear Michael,

What a long letter! What a detailed catalog of "bad things religion has done in history." Do you collect them? Are you trying out for the job of prosecuting attorney with God in the dock? That was unfair; I should have said "with religion in the dock," but I'll let the correctable version stand. (*God in the Dock* is the title of a book of essays by C. S. Lewis, by the way.)

I'm not a historian, and I'm not familiar with half of your examples, so I don't know for sure which ones are simply true, which are simply false, and which are half-truths or distortions of what really happened, except for the four most well-known examples: Galileo, the Spanish Inquisition, the Crusades, and the recent clerical sex abuse scandals. (You could have included the corrupt Renaissance popes; that would have made an even more scandalous case.) But most of your examples come under the heading of your next objection, the accusation that "religion promotes terrorism, oppression, witch hunts, inquisitions, and crusades—in nearly all times, places, and cultures, throughout history in empirical fact and therefore apparently by its inherent nature." So I think we have to take these two objections together, even though they're different in that the first one blames the believers and the second one blames the belief.

First of all, you make no attempt to look at the other side of the historical story, namely all the many good things, both general and specific, that religion has done in history, in fostering justice, compassion, peace, happiness, and so on. Even atheistic psychiatrists often recommend religion to their patients for the good it does them. One could make at least as long and heavy a list of goods as of evils. And then how would we judge this seesaw?

I think I already refuted the objection that a perfectly good God would not allow *any evil at all*, since that would remove free will; so you'd have to specify *how much* evil done by religious people refutes God. And how could you draw a line to do that? If the Holocaust of six million refutes God, why not a traffic accident that kills six? Why not one? Why not one robbery? Why not one hemorrhoid?

Second, the four most famous examples (Galileo, Crusades, Inquisition, and sex scandals) all do indeed count against religion. There was certainly serious moral as well as intellectual error on the part of religious people in condemning Galileo, in burning heretics, in the methods the Crusades used to reconquer the Holy Land from the Muslims, and in priests buggering little boys' bodies and souls. (I'd say the last one is even worse than the other three.)

But Galileo was a stubborn prima donna himself, though he was right in his science; and all the church wanted him to admit was that his theory was a *theory*. Copernicus had argued for the same theory earlier and not only got into no trouble with the church at all for teaching it but was actually supported, both politically and financially, by the church. It was, of course, an embarrassingly stupid mistake for the narrow-minded bishops to refuse to look through Galileo's telescope. But they were not the whole church.

We do indeed have "a similar situation with Darwin and evolution today." But the Catholic Church has no objection to evolution by natural selection as a scientific hypothesis, as long as it does not pretend to be a metaphysics that claims to refute the existence of God and the existence of souls. How could evolution disprove souls? Souls leave no fossils.

The Inquisition cleared the vast majority of its prisoners. The total number executed, in all the centuries the Inquisition existed, was far less than nearly all the earlier estimates. The trials were usually done with great care and fairness. The problem was the closeness of church and state, religion and politics. Religious heresy was also political sedition. That's why it was the Spanish state, not the church, that executed heretics. The church just defined the heresies, which is part of her job. Unfortunately, she also did part of the dirty work of the state in "handing over" heretics for execution. The idea that you could destroy heresies by destroying heretics was stupid, but no more stupid than the currently popular idea that in order to embrace heretics you have to embrace their heresies. Both ages make the same confusion between heretics and heresies. Both forget that we have to love heretics and sinners more and love heresies and sins less. (Science has heretics too, of course, for instance, "young earth creationists.")

That's not to exonerate the Inquisition, of course, just to lessen the charge. Guilty, but not as charged.

The Crusades were a defensive, not offensive, war. Muslim aggression had conquered the Christian Holy Land; the Crusaders only wanted to get it back. If that was not a just war, what war ever was? But as in most wars, just or unjust, atrocities were committed, most famously the sack of Constantinople—which, by the way, was condemned by the pope with utmost severity.

There is no defense of the recent clerical sex abuse scandals. Two things should be added, though. First, other institutions, both religious (other denominations and religions) and secular (e.g., the public school system) has at least as large a percentage of abusers as the Catholic Church. Second, the intellectual villain was not conservative, traditional religion but the new "liberal," modernist, "nonjudgmental" psychology that cleared most abusive priests for continued "service" after they were caught. That's no justification for pragmatic bishops who recycled the abusers.

As for "the war between religion and science," I challenge you to show me a single scientific discovery that has ever contradicted and refuted a single religious dogma. There is no such war. It is a myth. The only war is between bad science and bad religion, or bad scientists and bad religionists. Many religious people have often been stupidly and unfairly antiscientific, but many scientific people have also often been stupidly and unfairly antireligious.

As far as the literal wars that you blame on religion, all the worst, most murderous totalitarian dictators of the twentieth century were passionately antireligious: Hitler, Stalin, Mao, Pol Pot, Castro. And there have been more people martyred for their religious belief in the twentieth century than in all previous centuries in human history.

My bottom line summary is that religion has done a little evil and a lot of good while antireligion has done a little good and a lot of evil. Your historical summary is apparently the opposite. Both claims are so sweeping, and the data is so varied and detailed, that it seems impossible to do even prima facie justice to it in a few letters.

Finally, if you claim that "belief in absolutes tends to make you a tyrant," you are refuted both by tyrants who explicitly base their tyranny on relativism (like Mussolini) and saints whose absolutism makes them the opposite of tyrants. Besides, even mathematicians believe in absolutes; are they tyrants?

So should we talk about sex next?

Your friend,

Peter

42

Dear Michael,

Your last argument against religion is very simple: that it suppresses natural sex and the happiness it brings.

My answer could be equally simple: it doesn't. Religious people have happier sex lives than nonreligious people, according to the polls. (Also, married people are happier with their sex lives than unmarried people, according to the polls.)

Which is exactly what you would expect if God invented sex. Everything works better and makes us happier when it's used according to its nature and design, as established by its inventor. And if God is the designer, then following His design and His will equals following the essential nature of the thing, and that in turn equals success and happiness, in every field.

And if not, not. If sex is not designed by God, like a book, then it's like a blank book and we can write whatever meanings we want into it.

I count seven different but related questions that you ask in the course of your long letter of prosecution. I summarize them this way:

(1) Why should there be such a close connection between religion and sex so that religious sexual morality is always stricter

than nonreligious sexual morality? (Quick answer: because sex is holy because it's part of "the image of God," which is love between persons, and also because sex produces the only things in the universe with eternal and intrinsic value, human beings.)

(2) Why does religion see sex as primarily for procreation rather than for pleasure and intimacy and love? Why is it so *biological*? (Quick answer: because souls and bodies are related not like ghosts and houses but like the meaning of a poem and the words of the poem.)

(3) Why does religion (especially Catholicism) absolutize and permanentize marriage and sexual fidelity and demonize adultery and divorce? (Quick answer: because God did, when He invented it. See Mt 19:3–9.)

(4) Why would God put such severe strictures on the thing He Himself invented and attached such ecstatic pleasure to? (Quick answer: because the better a thing is, the more important it is to get it right and the more destructive it is to get it wrong.)

(5) If God does not exist, what follows about the sexual revolution? What secular imperatives should modify the sexual revolution, if any? (Quick answer: that's for you to say, not me. You're the rebel; I'm the establishment you rebelled against.)

(6) Why do religions, especially Catholicism, say so many sexual nos and so few yeses? Masturbation, fornication, homosexuality, "casual" consensual sex, even contraception—all sex is wrong except sex between one man and one woman, legally married, for life, intending children. And even there I'll bet the church says that most experimentation is wrong, for example, anal sex or oral sex or anything else that's "weird" but stimulating. (Quick answer: see number 4.)

(7) Obviously there's something more going on here than meets the eye. What's the hidden presupposition, the "big picture" or "metanarrative" that explains all this? And why can't religion spell it out, as it spells out its reasons for God and morality and life after death to the public with at least somewhat rational arguments? There's got to be a single ultimate psychological source of all this suppression and unsexiness, because it goes so contrary to our natural instincts for pleasure and freedom. (Quick answer: what looks like "unsexiness" to you is really sex to the max, designer sex, sex *au naturel*.)

Let's take your last and biggest question first. Isn't it possible that it's the world, or at least that relatively small spatiotemporal part of it that we call "modern Western civilization," that's obsessed with sex rather than the church? Like a drug addict teenager who accuses his parents of being "hung up on the issue" of drugs because they occasionally dare to remind him that he's being self-destructive?

I think the most radical difference between the religious and the secular view of sex comes from the religious doctrines of sin and the Fall. Secularists tell us to "accept ourselves as we are," but religion tells us that we're stupid, self-destructive sinners and that our present nature is fallen, unnatural, and abnormal.

Why do I call this "abnormalism" radical? Well, suppose there was a school of physics that held that there used to be a fifth fundamental force in the universe that reordered and reintegrated everything in the universe, starting with the four forces we now recognize, in a new and unimaginable way; and that that's why we've never found the "theory of everything" or the "unified field theory": because matter itself, all matter, is now in an abnormal condition and needs to be realigned by this missing fifth force to make the whole physical universe perfect and perfectly fit for human habitation.

You are probably thinking: good grief, my friend is a fundamentalist who believes in talking snakes and magic apples. No, the Fall story is highly symbolic, but it's historical, it's about us. Its *point* is not symbolic: that we are now abnormal, not normal, especially in our consciousness, which is stupid and self-deceptive, and above all in our heart, our desires, our loves, which are now selfish. We now naturally love ourselves more than, and even to the exclusion of, our neighbors and even God. (In sex, that's the difference between love and lust: the difference between unselfish and selfish love.) It's hard to pray, hard to give, hard to be a saint. That situation has to be abnormal. The good God could not have created us in such a condition where we need commandments to tell us to do what ought to be instinctive and full of joy and where we have a hell of a time obeying them. Our road up the mountain is too steep for our poor legs to make it: isn't it just as reasonable to blame the legs as to blame the road?

If you once accept this change of perspective, everything else in religious morality makes a lot more sense, especially when it comes to sexual morality. And there are some clues, even now, as to its truth, most notably the happiness of great saints and the unhappiness of great sinners. If religion is unnatural and oppressive to human nature and human happiness, we should expect to find the opposite.

Do you want to talk about this fundamental principle first, or do want to explore how it answers your other six questions? I have the burden of proof; you have the burden of the agenda.

Your friend,

Peter

43

Dear Michael,

Yes, I thought you'd want to explore the fundamental thing first, even though it's not as titillating as the other questions.

You ask how the Fall can be historical without being literal. The *fact* is literal—mankind was created perfect and innocent and freely chose to fall into sin and selfishness and folly—but the words and images of the story are not. Premodern, prescientific history is often told that way, for example, "George Washington was the father of his country."

And my reason for accepting the historicity of the Fall is not just the authority of the Bible and the church. Monogenism—the descent of the whole human race from one original couple—has never been scientifically proved (though genetics points in that direction, doesn't it?) but it's never been disproved either. And *somebody* must have come first, even if they were Ug and Glug from Madagascar instead of Adam and Eve from Eden (the names are symbolic). At some first point, water boils, and then it also begins to Boyle (obey Boyle's law for the behavior of gases, not liquids). (I've got pundicitis.) Once there were no creatures with self-consciousness and free moral choice; then there were.

162

There are also at least two essential theological reasons for taking the Fall as history. First, if there was no historical Fall, but it's only a timeless archetype in a mythical story, then there need not be a historical incarnation and redemption either, only an archetype in a mythical story. If there was no historical Adam, there's no need for a historical Christ, whom Paul calls "the second Adam." And second, if there was no Fall from perfect innocence, then God created us with these sinful habits and desires as we now have them, in which case He is causally, directly responsible for our sinfulness.

As to the psychological question of what could possibly have motivated two perfectly happy and innocent people to choose evil over good, disobedience over obedience, read C. S. Lewis's fantasy novel *Perelandra* about an alternative world in which the Fall *didn't* happen but almost did.

And if you share the common cavil about the doctrine of Original Sin (which means our present habitual love of selfishness, not Adam's first actual sin) being insultingly pessimistic and negative in its anthropology, I quote Chesterton again when he said that Original Sin is the only Christian dogma that can be proved just by reading the newspapers.

Now for the big picture. Start with God as love. (That's the reason He's the Trinity, by the way: a single person can't give unselfish love until he has another person to give it to. And if that other is not divine but human, then God needs us in order for Him to be love, and before He created and/or evolved us, He was not love.)

True love means giving the gift of self to another. "I love *you*" means "I love you for you, not for me." It's self-forgetful. We experience moments of this self-forgetfulness, or "ecstasy" (which means literally "standing outside yourself"), when we fall totally in love with another person of the opposite sex. That's one of the ways in which sex is holy and a foretaste of heaven. It's part of "the image of God" according to the Bible (Gn 1:27). Its oneness in otherness images the Trinity's oneness in otherness.

So all the fuss about sex is not because we have a low view of it, as inherently selfish, animalistic, and materialistic. Exactly the opposite. You put taboos around temples, not outhouses.

Sex is also holy because it naturally produces new *persons*. It's called "the reproductive system," for heaven's sake! And that's why contraception is wrong: because it's saying to God, "We don't want You here creating a new, infinitely valuable image of Yourself. We're locking the door so you don't come in and do Your miracle of creating a new eternal soul when we provide the body for it. We're like priests saying Mass for fun but not wanting Your real presence to come at the moment of consecration, so we're going to fake the words 'This is My Body' instead of saying them."

You see, those two moments—biological conception and spiritual consecration, or what Catholics call transubstantiation—are the holiest moments in time because God continually creates miracles at those two moments; and those two places—a woman's body and a Catholic altar—are the two holiest places in the world because that's where He does it. Of course, I know you don't believe that—you're not even a theist, much less a Catholic—but you can at least understand it and understand what consequences follow about sex if one does believe it.

For instance, take the condemnation of masturbation. Masturbation is "natural" in the sense of being nearly universal, so why is it wrong? Because it's unnatural in undoing what God designed sex to do: to take us out of ourselves into another person, in body and soul. It substitutes your fantasy other for the real other, which is really substituting yourself for the other, self-love for other-love: exactly the opposite of what sex is supposed to do. Those fantasy lovers never bitch, quarrel, protest, sleep, or fart. They don't take you out of yourself but into yourself. They reverse the real path to wisdom and joy.

Of course, as an atheist you will probably say there is no such thing as "what sex is supposed to do" (or what *anything* is supposed to do, including us) if there is no designing mind of God to "suppose" it. Teleology, or real purpose and design, real objective ends—what Aristotle called "final causality"—fits into the theistic worldview much better than into the atheistic one. Some philosophers claim that design in nature can prove theism, others deny that; some claim "intelligent design" presupposes theism, others deny that; but all agree that it it *fits* the theistic worldview as music or humor fit human nature. Aristotle was not a theist but a deist—his God didn't design, create, love, interact with, or even know the world—yet he instinctively "saw" final causality everywhere. He just didn't draw out its theistic implications, as the argument from design does.

The "existential" problem with the atheist worldview is that if nothing has an inherent, objectively real purpose, then neither do we. So all purposes are man-made, artificial rather than natural, subjective rather than objective in origin. But the creator of a thing has authority over his creation; so if there is no God, but *we* created all purposes, then we also created our own purpose— which could be anything we create and design it to be: sadism or Nazism or cannibalism or suicide or anything else at all. If sex has no inherent, objective, natural end and purpose because nothing

166 Peter Kreeft

does, then neither do we. If we do—if there is any sense at all in asking the question "What is the meaning of life?"—then everything else does too, including sex.

Unless, of course, we are such aliens that we are the only meaningfully designed creatures in a universe of meaningless, arbitrary chance. But who or what designed us if there is no God? Did the meaningless and unintelligent universe "design" our meaning?

I don't know whether this amounts to a logically compelling proof. But it shows the price you have to pay for atheism and implicitly asks you why you would pay it. What makes it worthwhile giving up all the things you have to give up to be an atheist, such as a real, objectively true meaning and design to both nature and your own life?

That's how I see it. Since you are an atheist, that can't be how you see it. So I still don't understand why you see it otherwise. I've tried to explain the "perks" of theism. Now I think it's your turn to explain the perks of atheism. Including the existential perks, since we've already discussed all the main logical ones, I think. (Or have we?) So can I put the burden of proof on you for a bit?

Your friend,
Peter

44

Dear Michael,

You never cease to surprise me. I expected more arguments about sex, or about other moral issues, or about scientific issues that you promised (or threatened) to go back to, like "the emergence of consciousness from natural selection." I did not expect this candid confession:

> I still think none of your arguments is demonstrative, and though I've never met you, I think it's not likely that you're not a saint like Francis who could spiritually woo me into sharing his faith. And I think I understand all the arguments we have exchanged, on both sides, quite clearly, and I am not convinced by your arguments, though you express them very well. So why is the result of this exchange of letters a state of confusion in my mind? And why do I refuse to call my present state of mind either theism, atheism, or even agnosticism? Perhaps I should call it an agnosticism about everything, even agnosticism.

My first answer to your question about your present state of mind will, I think, surprise *you*, as you have often surprised me. I think it will surprise you because it comes from an absent-minded

167

philosophy professor who loves to argue abstractions and who tends to ignore personal, psychological, and emotional issues. My answer comes from another little paragraph in your last letter. Perhaps you can suddenly see the connection, how it can cast light on your present state of mind. You wrote: "I was liberated from my neck brace today. Now I understand what the prisoners in Plato's cave must have felt like when they took off their chains and turned their necks around. What freedom!"

You are still in the cave, but now you are at least free to turn your head. If this is agnosticism, isn't it more liberating than atheism? And if atheism is like a neck brace, and if there are no compelling reasons not to take it off and look around—

Doesn't science teach us over and over again that "there are more things in heaven and earth than are dreamed of in your philosophy"?

I don't know what to say next. I have no agenda to impose on you, just an invitation to follow your own pointing fingers that seem to lead to exits from the cave. If you want to talk about these paths (which Plato calls "steep and rocky") I am happy to be your friend as you explore and evaluate them. In fact, I am happy to be your friend anywhere, even if you stay inside the cave.

Your friend,

Peter

45

Dear Michael,

Still another delightful surprise! What a fortunate coincidence that you are going to Martha's Vineyard next week! From my point of view you are not just "going" but "coming"—did you know that I own a little cottage there? You absolutely must come and stay with us at least over Labor Day weekend. I will show you good fishing and good beaches and good waves (September is the best month for them), and I will initiate you into the world's cheapest and easiest mystical experience, surfing. Anyone, even an old fogie and a landlubber, can learn to do it in one afternoon with a bodyboard. (I have six!) The sea will drown many sorrows and wash many wounds. It can do that better than philosophers can.

And we will talk late into the cool nights. The best things in life are free, like conversations about important things between friends. There has to be many more good ones to come. We've just begun to scratch the surface.

Your friend,
Peter

ABOUT THE AUTHOR

Peter Kreeft is professor of philosophy at Boston College. He has published more than seventy books in philosophy and religion, including Socratic dialogs with Descartes, Hume, Kant, Freud, Kierkegaard, Machiavelli, Marx, and Sartre; textbooks in logic and the history of philosophy; and books on death, heaven, Catholicism, suffering, abortion, love, apologetics, surfing, Jesus, C. S. Lewis, Aquinas, and Pascal. He loves his five grandchildren, four children, one wife, one cat, and one God.